Table of Contents
Spelling Homework Booklet
Grade 3

Where Have All the Vowels Gone?

Use the clue in parentheses to fill in the missing vowel for each word. Then write each word on the line.

1. w__nt (gone) _____

2. c__ndy (a sweet treat) _____

3. f__sh (a water animal) _____

4. kn__t (a knob in rope or string) _____

5. j__mp (leap or hop) _____

6. c__nt (a penny) _____

7. __nch (1/12 of a foot) _____

8. pl__s (add or also) _____

9. l__mp (gives off light) _____

10. b__x (a container) _____

11. qu__z (a short test) _____

12. fr__sh (new or recent) _____

13. l__ck (good fortune) _____

14. j__g (to run slowly) _____

15. s__ck (a bag) _____

Write each group of words in alphabetical order.

1. cent, box, candy

_____, _____, _____

2. inch, fresh, fish

_____, _____, _____

3. jump, jog, knot

_____, _____, _____

4. luck, plus, lamp

_____, _____, _____

5. went, quiz, sack

_____, _____, _____

Change the underlined letter(s) to make a word used above.

6. w i s h _____

7. w a n t _____

8. t e n t _____

9. j u g _____

10. s o c k _____

11. l u m p _____

12. k n i t _____

13. l a s t _____

14. l o c k _____

15. h a n d y _____

Vowels for Sale

It's your turn to "buy" a vowel. Choose the correct vowel to make a word. Then write it in the empty box.

vowels 5¢

1. / $\bar{a}$ /or / $\bar{i}$ /

| c | | p | e |

2. / $\bar{u}$ /or / $\bar{i}$ /

| d | r | | v | e |

3. / $\bar{i}$ /or / $\bar{u}$ /

| w | h | | t | e |

4. / $\bar{e}$ /or / $\bar{u}$ /

| h | | g | e |

5. / $\bar{a}$ /or / $\bar{o}$ /

| n | | s | e |

6. / $\bar{a}$ /or / $\bar{u}$ /

| g | r | | d | e |

7. / $\bar{i}$ /or / $\bar{u}$ /

| s | h | | n | e |

8. / $\bar{a}$ /or / $\bar{o}$ /

| p | | g | e |

9. / $\bar{e}$ /or / $\bar{a}$ /

| g | r | | p | e |

10. / $\bar{u}$ /or / $\bar{i}$ /

| c | | b | e |

11. / $\bar{a}$ /or / $\bar{i}$ /

| s | | f | e |

12. / $\bar{u}$ /or / $\bar{e}$ /

| c | | t | e |

13. / $\bar{a}$ /or / $\bar{i}$ /

| o | u | t | s | | d | e |

14. / $\bar{a}$ /or / $\bar{u}$ /

| m | | n | e |

15. / $\bar{i}$ /or / $\bar{o}$ /

| e | n | v | e | l | | p | e |

Analogies are comparisons of words.
For example: piglet is to sow as chick is to hen .
Or: green is to greenish as red is to reddish .

Complete these analogies.

1. Foot is to toes, as face is to _____.

2. Up is to down, as inside is to _____.

3. Shone is to shine, as drove is to _____.

4. Prune is to plum, as raisin is to _____.

5. Hat is to head, as _____ is to shoulders.

6. Circle is to ball, as square is to _____.

7. Hair is to person, as _____ is to horse.

8. Book is to bookbag, as letter is to _____.

9. Ugly is to ogre, as _____ is to baby.

10. Star is to twinkle, as sun is to _____.

11. Grass is to green, as snow is to _____.

12. Little is to big, as tiny is to _____.

13. Branch is to tree, as _____ is to book.

14. Student is to pupil, as score is to _____.

15. Unhappy is to happy, as unsafe is to _____.

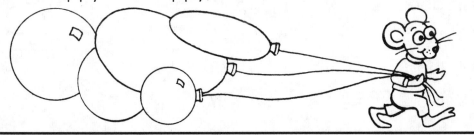

When Two Vowels Go Walking...

In these words, the first vowel has a long sound and the second vowel is silent. Write the letter of the correct pronunciation for each word. The first one is done for you.

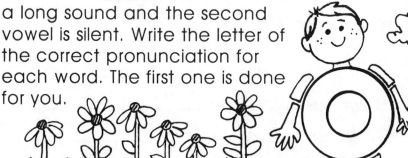

1. paid __e__   a. /chān/

2. goes ___   b. /tēch/

3. dream ___   c. /snāl/

4. chain ___   d. /pī/

5. meal ___   e. /pād/

6. teach ___   f. /thrōt/

7. weed ___   g. /lī/

8. street ___   h. /wēd/

9. snail ___   i. /drēm/

10. lie ___   j. /lōd/

11. throat ___   k. /tōst/

12. doe ___   l. /mēl/

13. toast ___   m. /gōz/

14. load ___   n. /dō/

15. pie ___   o. /strēt/

Guide words are used in a dictionary to let you know the first and last words on the page. Write each of the words from page 6 in alphabetical order under the correct set of guide words.

apple   guess

_____

_____

_____

_____

hammer   nurse

_____

_____

_____

_____

often   sweet

_____

_____

_____

_____

tail   which

_____

_____

_____

_____

You are playing a word game, and these are your seven tiles. Which two words on page 6 could you make with them?

_____ or _____

Brad's Blender

Drop in the right letters and out come perfectly "blended" words! Use the clues to unscramble each group of letters to make a word.

HINT! Each word begins with one of these consonant blends:

bl	br	cl	cr	dr	fl	fr	gr	pl	sl	sm	st	sw	gl	tr

1. u r t t h   (not false) _____
2. e e s t w   (tasting sugary) _____
3. d s t u y   (to learn) _____
4. a l l m s   (not big) _____
5. e e l p s   (dream time) _____
6. e l n p t y   (lots and lots) _____
7. g o u p r   (a set) _____
8. f o n r t   (opposite of back) _____
9. e f l o r w   (part of a plant) _____
10. a c r y z   (mixed-up or silly) _____
11. a e c l n   (not dirty) _____
12. b h r s u   (tool for painting) _____
13. b c k l o   (piece of wood) _____
14. d i k n r   (to sip liquid) _____
15. l g d e i   (move smoothly) _____

Use a word from page 8 to complete each sentence.

1. Laura carved a _____ of wood into a seagull.
2. Mrs. Mead showed the class how to use the paint _____.
3. There are five students in my math _____.
4. Jenny gave her teacher a red _____.
5. You'll have to _____ your words to pass the test.
6. A lion is large, but a mouse is _____.
7. It is always wise to tell the _____.
8. The opposite of bitter is _____.
9. Spring is a good time to thoroughly _____ the house.
10. Jill likes to _____ apple cider.
11. Jon needs to sit in the _____ until he gets his new glasses.
12. It sounds _____, but I love to iron.
13. Scott likes to _____ late on Sundays.
14. I have _____ of paper in my desk.
15. Watch the skater _____ across the ice.

CHALLENGE: See how many other words you can rhyme with the words below. Score one point for each word that begins with a single consonant and two points for each that begins with a consonant blend. Can you make 12 points?

brush   drink   block

And in Closing...

Cross off the last letter of each word. Add the consonant blend in parentheses and write the new word on the line. The first one has been done for you.

CHAIRMAN

FIRST ANNUAL CONVENTION OF CONSONANT BLENDS

1. cod (st) **cost**

2. as (nt) _____

3. mop (st) _____

4. ten (st) _____

5. set (lf) _____

6. won (lf) _____

7. mid (lk) _____

8. fin (lm) _____

9. cat (mp) _____

10. sat (nd) _____

11. pop (nd) _____

12. tad (sk) _____

13. map (sk) _____

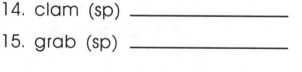

14. clam (sp) _____

15. grab (sp) _____

Our speaker wrote his speech in code. Use the key to decode the words listed below. Write each one on the line and circle the consonant blend.

a	b	c	d	e	f	g	h	i	j	k	l	m
z	y	x	w	v	u	t	s	r	q	p	o	n

1. g z h p = _____ ta**sk** _____

2. k l m w = _____

3. x l h g = _____

4. u r o n = _____

5. h v o u = _____

6. z m g = _____

7. h z m w = _____

8. t i z h k = _____

9. n z h p = _____

10. x z n k = _____

11. n l h g = _____

12. n r o p = _____

13. x o z h k = _____

14. d l o u = _____

15. g v h g = _____

CHALLENGE: Use the key to write your name in the secret code.

_____

Left-Out Letters

Super Sleuth is hot on the trail of stray letters. For each pair of words choose a contraction from the Word List and write it on the line. Then write the letter(s) left out in the boxes. The first one is done for you.

Word List				
can't	don't	you're	that's	I'll
haven't	doesn't	we're	what's	they've
couldn't	I'm	they're	we'll	you've

1. I am _____ I'm _____ ☐ a

2. that is _____ ☐

3. they have _____ ☐ ☐

4. can not _____ ☐ ☐

5. have not _____ ☐

6. what is _____ ☐

7. you are _____ ☐

8. we are _____ ☐

9. could not _____ ☐

10. they are _____ ☐

11. we will _____ ☐ ☐

12. you have _____ ☐ ☐

13. do not _____ ☐

14. I will _____ ☐ ☐

15. does not _____ ☐

Write a contraction that makes sense in each
sentence.

I'm   we're   couldn't   we'll   they've

1. I _____ go to school today.
2. I'm sure _____ be able to go along.
3. _____ going to go on a picnic!
4. Dad says that _____ the best pitcher on
   the team.
5. I know that _____ wanted to go for a
   long time.

that's   can't   you're   you've   doesn't

6. He _____ like spaghetti!
7. I think _____ the funniest thing I've ever
   heard!
8. Everybody knows _____ the best reader in
   the class.
9. I know _____ worked hard all year.
10. I _____ believe what you're telling me!

haven't   what's   they're   don't   I'll

11. _____ your dog's name?
12. If I study, _____ do well on the test.
13. I think _____ going to the store.
14. I _____ done the dishes yet.
15. I _____ want to go!

Love That Calendar Girl!

Write the months of the year
in alphabetical order.

1. _____

2. _____

3. _____

4. _____

5. _____

6. _____

7. _____

8. _____

9. _____

10. _____

11. _____

12. _____

Unscramble each of the "calendar"
words below.

13. a e r y _____

14. e e k w _____

15. a d y _____

16. a a e c d l n r _____

17. h m n o t _____

January
February
March
April
May
June
July
August
September
October
November
December

14

Use a word from page 12 to complete each sentence.

1. Independence Day is always on _____fourth.

2. The month of _____ never has more than twenty-nine days.

3. _____ is the month for Thanksgiving.

4. Mother's Day is on the second Sunday in

   _____.

5. Every _____ contains twenty-four hours.

6. In _____ we celebrate St. Patrick's Day.

7. Each new year begins with the month of

   _____.

8. Use a _____ to keep track of the

   days, weeks, and months in a _____.

9. The month of _____ brings Labor Day and the beginning of school.

10. _____ is the fourth month of the calendar year.

11. Christmas and Hanukkah are celebrated in

    _____.

12. _____ is a month for graduations and Father's Day.

13. The _____ of September always has thirty days.

14. We celebrate Columbus Day in _____.

15. The eighth month of the calendar year is

    _____.

16. There are seven days in a _____.

Review

Pages 2-5 Write each word under the correct heading.

jog   white   nose

grape   cent   fresh

inch   shine   mine

cute   lamp   candy

Long Vowel Words   ### Short Vowel Words

_____   _____

_____   _____

_____   _____

_____   _____

_____   _____

_____   _____

Pages 6-7 Circle the vowels in each word that make the long sound.

chain   toast   goes

teach   dream   paid

lie   meal   throat

Pages 8-11 Circle the consonant blends in the following words.

clean   sand   most

sweet   glide   group

mask   test   milk

Pages 12-13 Write contractions for the following word pairs.

do not _____ you are _____

can not _____ they are _____

that is _____ I am _____

I will _____ we are _____

Pages 14-15 Circle the misspelled word in each group and write it correctly on the line.

January Febuary April _____

huge calender knot _____

munth envelope cent _____

February October wite _____

Desember went year _____

March jog Novembr _____

September Oktober calendar _____

Cheers for the Chief

Use the clues to choose a consonant digraph to complete each word. Then write the word on the line. The first one is done for you.

ch	sh	th	qu	wh

1. not a boo, but a <u>c</u> <u>h</u> e e r   **cheer**
2. not a brave, but the __ __ i e f   _____
3. not a minnow, but a __ __ a l e   _____
4. not in the light, but in the __ __ a d o w s

   _____
5. not a cape, but a __ __ a w l   _____
6. not a blanket, but a __ __ i l t   _____
7. not thick, but __ __ i n   _____
8. not Halloween, but __ __ a n k s g i v i n g

   _____
9. not noisy, but __ __ i e t   _____
10. not dull, but __ __ a r p   _____
11. not a crayon, but a piece of __ __ a l k

    _____
12. not a 4-leaf clover, but a __ __ a m r o c k

    _____
13. not keeping, but __ __ a r i n g   _____
14. not a part, but a __ __ o l e   _____
15. not wasteful, but __ __ r i f t y   _____

Replace the underlined letter(s) with a consonant digraph that makes a word from page 18.

1. c̲ a r i n g _____

2. s̲ k̲ i n _____

3. t̲ h̲ i e f _____

4. t̲ a l k _____

5. t̲ i l t _____

6. m̲ a l e _____

7. m̲ o l e _____

8. c̲ r a w l _____

9. p̲ e e r _____

10. c̲ a r p _____

Fill in the boxes with the words from page 18 that you did not use above. Next to each, write other words that begin with the some consonant digraph.

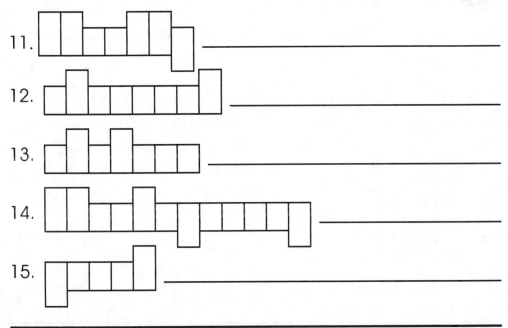

11. _____

12. _____

13. _____

14. _____

15. _____

Get Wise About Long "Eyes"

Use the clues and the beginning letter(s) in parentheses to make words with the / i / sound. The first one is done for you.

1. airplane ride . . . .(fl) _____**flight**_____

2. not dim . . . .(br)_____

3. unable to see . . . .(bl)_____

4. opposite of wrong . . . .(r)_____

5. not tame . . . .(w)_____

6. pesty black insects . . . .(fl)_____

7. not an adult . . . .(ch)_____

8. gentle, kind; not harsh . . . .(m)_____

9. to locate something lost . . . .(f)_____

10. make up your_____ . . . .(m)_____

11. opposite of laughs . . . .(cr)_____

12. plural of try . . . .(tr)_____

Add a **y** to each pair of letters to make a word with the / i / sound. Write the word on the line.

13. | s | p | | _____

14. | t | r | | _____

15. | w | h | | _____

Write words from page 20 that rhyme with each word.

fight

1. _____

2. _____

3. _____

kind

4. _____

5. _____

6. _____

spies

7. _____

8. _____

9. _____

fly

10. _____

11. _____

12. _____

Write the words from page 20 that you did not use above.

13. _____

14. _____

15. _____

CHALLENGE: Can you think of other words to rhyme with these words? Use a dictionary to check your spelling.

fight	kind	fly
_____	_____	_____
_____	_____	_____
_____	_____	_____

The Odd Couples

Write a word from the Word List to complete each puzzle. The first one is done for you.

Word List				
book	flour	auto	soil	moon
wood	count	because	coin	tooth
foot	mouth	sauce	noise	loose

1. louse − ou + oo = __loose__

2. boot − t + k = _____

3. soul − ou + oi = _____

4. spoon − sp + m = _____

5. nose − o + oi = _____

6. wool − l + d = _____

7. tool − l + th = _____

8. cent − e + ou = _____

9. become − ome + ause = _____

10. floor − oo + ou = _____

11. fool − l + t = _____

12. coil − l + n = _____

13. south − s + m = _____

14. Pluto − Pl + a = _____

15. soot − oot + auce = _____

Fill in each blank with a word from page 22.

1. Rebecca planted the seed in a pot of

   _____.

2. The button on my coat is _____.

3. Another word for _____ is car.

4. Matt broke his _____ playing football.

5. Close your _____ when chewing food.

6. You use _____ to make pie dough.

7. Mrs. Bradford had an old, gold _____
   called a doubloon.

8. Brennan lost a front _____ in school.

9. Joel looked at the _____ through his
   telescope.

10. Dad is chopping _____ for the
    fireplace.

11. Meg's favorite _____ is *Tuck
    Everlasting*.

12. Michael likes barbeque _____ on his
    hamburger.

13. The car is making a strange _____.

14. One should always _____ one's
    blessings.

15. Rob likes pizza _____ it tastes so good.

Looking for Double Trouble

Double the final consonant of each word in parentheses and add **ed** or **ing** so that the sentence makes sense. Write the word on the line.

1. The chocolate (drip) _____ all over the ice cream.

2. Amy's cat is (rub) _____ its head against my leg.

3. Bill is (set) _____ the table.

4. Mother (thin) _____ the soup with water.

5. Jason has a (spot) _____ dog.

6. Meg (ship) _____ a gift to her cousin.

7. The hare (hop) _____ across the field.

8. Krista spent the day (shop) _____ .

9. Eric made noise (drum) _____ his drums.

10. Aaron (slip) _____ on a patch of ice.

11. Dad (jog) _____ around the block.

12. Our dog (beg) _____ for a piece of pizza.

13. Is Matt (gab) _____ on the phone?

14. Beth is (sit) _____ in the rocking chair.

15. Jenna's favorite sport is (swim) _____ .

Dividing these words into syllables *really* isn't difficult. Just separate the words between the double consonants! The first one is done for you.

1. shopping   <u>shop</u>   <u>ping</u>

2. spotted   _____   _____

3. sitting   _____   _____

4. drumming   _____   _____

5. rubbing   _____   _____

6. swimming   _____   _____

7. setting   _____   _____

8. gabbing   _____   _____

Double the final consonant and add **ed** before writing each word. Circle **d** if the final sound is the sound of /*d*/ or **t** if the final sound is the sound of /*t*/.

9. drip   _____   d   t

10. ship   _____   d   t

11. beg   _____   d   t

12. slip   _____   d   t

13. thin   _____   d   t

14. hop   _____   d   t

15. jog   _____   d   t

Sh! The Consonants Are Sleeping

Circle the silent consonant in each word. Write the word in the correct word box.

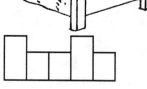

1. w a l k
2. j u d g e
3. f a s t e n
4. c o u l d
5. k n i f e
6. w r i t e
7. b r i d g e
8. h a l f
9. l o d g e
10. e d g e
11. s h o u l d
12. t h u m b
13. w a t c h
14. s i g n
15. w r o n g

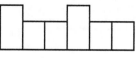
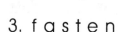

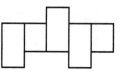
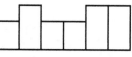
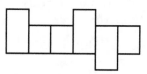
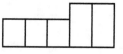

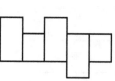
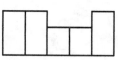

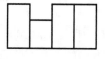
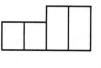
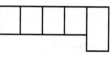

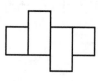

Fill in the silent consonant and write each word on the line. Then find each word in the wordsearch.

1. ha__f _____   9. e__ge _____

2. ju__ge _____   10. fas__en _____

3. wa__ch _____   11. __rong _____

4. cou__d _____   12. wa__k _____

5. thum__ _____   13. lo__ge _____

6. si__n _____   14. shou__d _____

7. __nife _____   15. bri__ge _____

8. __rite _____

Look across and down.

w	a	c	h	s	f	w	r	i	t	e	i	e	w
a	w	o	l	b	t	r	j	u	g	j	e	d	a
l	h	u	d	r	h	o	s	v	f	u	s	g	t
w	a	l	k	i	u	n	f	l	o	d	g	e	c
a	l	d	o	d	m	g	a	t	h	g	a	s	h
h	a	l	f	g	b	f	a	s	t	e	n	i	a
n	i	f	e	e	f	k	s	o	u	r	s	g	f
k	n	i	f	e	g	s	h	o	u	l	d	n	f

Stuck in the Middle

Draw lines to match the beginning and ending of a word with the consonant digraph in the middle. Then write the word.

no   ck   y _____

lu   ng   ing ___**nothing**___

si   th   le _____

---

kit   ch   er _____

ju   th   le _____

wea   ng   en _____

---

tele   ch   out _____

cat   ph   one _____

wi   th   er _____

---

no   wh   ere _____

work   sh   es _____

clo   th   op _____

---

pa   th   ward _____

ba   gh   ing _____

lau   ck   way _____

Divide each word into syllables. You may want to use a dictionary to check your work.

EXAMPLE:
brothers   **broth**   **ers**

1. laughing   _____   _____

2. kitchen   _____   _____

3. without   _____   _____

4. lucky   _____   _____

5. weather   _____   _____

6. workshop   _____   _____

7. nothing   _____   _____

8. catcher   _____   _____

9. backward   _____   _____

10. pathway   _____   _____

11. nowhere   _____   _____

12. telephone   _____ _____ _____

Circle the middle consonant digraph in each word, and then write the word.

13. j u n g l e _____

14. c l o t h e s _____

15. s i n g l e _____

For the Sport of It

Write the word that best fits each clue.

Word List			
coach	champions	soccer	pitcher
field	basketball	football	baseball
goalie	teammates	skating	tennis
score	touchdown	hockey	

1. game played with stick and puck _____
2. person who throws a ball to a batter _____
3. game played with racket and ball _____
4. person who guards the goal in soccer _____
5. game played with bat and ball _____
6. person who trains athletes _____
7. Michael Jordan's favorite sport _____
8. game played with oval-shaped ball _____
9. gliding along on rollers or blades _____
10. grassy area to play football or soccer _____
11. record of points made in a game _____
12. fellow members on a team _____
13. one way to score points in football _____
14. the first-place team _____
15. game in which ball is moved primarily by kicking

_____

In each group of words, circle the word that doesn't belong and write it on the line.

1. football, touchdown, goalie _____

2. hockey, basketball, skating _____

3. stick, puck, pitcher _____

4. football, batter, pitcher _____

5. score, bat, ball _____

6. coach, helmet, cap _____

7. bat, skating, ball _____

8. pitcher, baseball, touchdown _____

9. tennis, goalie, puck _____

10. skating, hockey, field _____

11. bat, ball, hockey _____

12. baseball, champions, soccer _____

13. teammates, field, court _____

14. touchdown, soccer, home run _____

15. baseball, touchdown, football _____

CHALLENGE: Use the Word List on page 30 to write the sport each group of words describes.

16. ice, skates, puck, stick, goalie _____

17. shortstop, catcher, batter, pitcher _____

18. touchdown, quarterback, field goal, kicker

_____

It's All in the Family

Draw a line to match two
words that go together best.
Write *both* words on the line.

1. mother   uncle _____

2. brother   niece _____

3. aunt   wife _____

4. son   adults _____

5. nephew   daughter _____

6. husband   father _____

7. children   sister _____

Write the word from the Word List that best fits each
sentence.

```
                    Word List
          cousin        parents
          babies        family
```

8. My father's niece is my _____ .

9. Mom and Dad are my _____ .

10. Our _____ has four members.

11. If Mom has twins, then we'll have two _____ .

        IF0136 Spelling

If the word below is singular, write its plural. If the word is plural, write its singular form.

1. husbands_____

2. nieces_____

3. child_____

4. sons_____

5. mothers_____

6. sisters_____

7. family_____

8. wives_____

9. cousins_____

10. aunts_____

11. fathers_____

12. brothers_____

13. baby_____

14. nephews_____

15. uncles_____

16. adult_____

17. parent_____

18. daughters_____

Review

Pages 18-21 Write each word. Circle the beginning consonant digraph and underline any / i / sound.

chief _____   quiet _____

shawl _____   sharp _____

child _____   whale _____

Pages 22-23 Use the Word List on page 22 to complete the crossword.

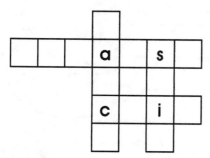

Pages 24-25 Write each word by adding **ed** and then **ing**.

beg   _____   _____

spot   _____   _____

thin   _____   _____

jog   _____   _____

Pages 26-27 Write the silent consonant in each word.

lo__ge   __rong   fas__en

wa__k   shou__d   __rite

thum__   ju__ge   wa__ch

Pages 28-29 Circle the consonant digraph in the middle of each word.

telephone   nothing   weather

kitchen   without   clothes

laughing   nowhere   lucky

Pages 30-33 Write each word and draw lines to divide each one into syllables.

pitcher _____

teammates _____

nephew _____

daughter _____

tennis _____

helmet _____

parents _____

The Mysterious Code

Super Sleuth is at work on a case. Use his key to decode each word. Use the Word List to check your spelling.

a	b	c	d	e	f	g	h	i	j	k	l	m
z	y	x	w	v	u	t	s	r	q	p	o	n

Word List

1. s f i i b = _____   garden

2. h x z i u = _____   birth

3. s v i w = _____   hurry

4. b z i w = _____   stories

5. m l i g s = _____   scarf

6. l i x s z i w = _____   force

7. u z i n = _____   turkey

8. y r i g s = _____   cartwheel

9. h g l i r v h = _____   herd

10. g f i p v b = _____   orange

11. u l i x v = _____   turn

12. t z i w v m = _____   north

13. g f i m = _____   orchard

14. x z i g d s v v o = _____   yard

15. l i z m t v = _____   farm

Answer Key

Spelling
Homework Booklet
Grade 3

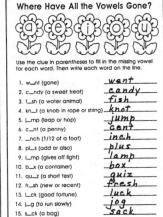

Where Have All the Vowels Gone?

Use the clue in parentheses to fill in the missing vowel for each word. Then write each word on the line.

1. w__nt (gone) — went
2. c__ndy (a sweet treat) — candy
3. f__sh (a water animal) — fish
4. kn__t (a knob in rope or string) — knot
5. l__mp (leap or hop) — jump
6. c__nt (a penny) — cent
7. __nch (1/12 of a foot) — inch
8. pl__s (add or also) — plus
9. l__mp (gives off light) — lamp
10. b__x (a container) — box
11. qu__z (a short test) — quiz
12. fr__sh (new or recent) — fresh
13. l__ck (good fortune) — luck
14. j__g (to run slowly) — jog
15. s__ck (a bag) — sack

©1992 Instructional Fair, Inc.   2   IF0136 Spelling

Write each group of words in alphabetical order.

1. cent, box, candy
   box   candy   cent
2. inch, fresh, fish
   fish   fresh   inch
3. jump, jog, knot
   jog   jump   knot
4. luck, plus, lamp
   lamp   luck   plus
5. went, quiz, sack
   quiz   sack   went

Change the underlined letter(s) to make a word used above.

6. wish — fish
7. want — went
8. tent — cent
9. jug — jog
10. sock — sack
11. lump — jump
12. knit — knot
13. last — lamp
14. lock — luck
15. handy — candy

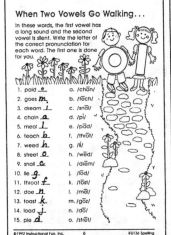

©1992 Instructional Fair, Inc.   3   IF0136 Spelling

Vowels for Sale

It's your turn to "buy" a vowel. Choose the correct vowel to make a word. Then write it in the empty box.

1. /ā/ or /ĭ/ — c a p e
2. /ū/ or /ĭ/ — d r i v e
3. /ĭ/ or /ū/ — wh i t e
4. /ē/ or /ū/ — h u g e
5. /ō/ or /ō/ — n o s e
6. /ā/ or /ū/ — g r a d e
7. /ĭ/ or /ū/ — s h i n e
8. /ĭ/ or /ū/ — p a g e
9. /ē/ or /ā/ — g r a p e
10. /ū/ or /ĭ/ — c u b e
11. /ā/ or /ĭ/ — s a f e
12. /ū/ or /ō/ — c u t e
13. /ō/ or /ĭ/ — o u t s i d e
14. /ā/ or /ū/ — m a n e
15. /ĭ/ or /ō/ — e n v e l o p e

©1992 Instructional Fair, Inc.   4   IF0136 Spelling

Analogies are comparisons of words.
For example: piglet is to sow as chick is to hen.
Or: green is to greenish as red is to reddish.

Complete these analogies.

1. Foot is to toes, as face is to — nose.
2. Up is to down, as inside is to — outside.
3. Shone is to shine, as drove is to — drive.
4. Prune is to plum, as raisin is to — grape.
5. Hat is to head, as cape is to shoulders.
6. Circle is to ball, as square is to — cube.
7. Hair is to person, as mane is to horse.
8. Book is to bookbag, as letter is to — envelope.
9. Ugly is to ogre, as cute is to baby.
10. Star is to twinkle, as sun is to — shine.
11. Grass is to green, as snow is to — white.
12. Little is to big, as tiny is to — huge.
13. Branch is to tree, as page is to book.
14. Student is to pupil, as score is to — grade.
15. Unhappy is to happy, as unsafe is to — safe.

©1992 Instructional Fair, Inc.   5   IF0136 Spelling

When Two Vowels Go Walking...

In these words, the first vowel has a long sound and the second vowel is silent. Write the letter of the correct pronunciation for each word. The first one is done for you.

1. paid — e — a. /chān/
2. goes — m — b. /tēch/
3. dream — a — c. /snāl/
4. chain — a — d. /pī/
5. meal — l — e. /pād/
6. teach — b — f. /thrōt/
7. weed — h — g. /lī/
8. street — o — h. /wēd/
9. snail — c — i. /dīēm/
10. lie — g — j. /lōd/
11. throat — f — k. /tōst/
12. doe — h — l. /māl/
13. toast — k — m. /gōz/
14. load — j — n. /dōl/
15. pie — d — o. /strēt/

©1992 Instructional Fair, Inc.   6   IF0136 Spelling

Guide words are used in a dictionary to let you know the first and last words on the page. Write each of the words from page 6 in alphabetical order under the correct set of guide words.

apple	guess		hammer	nurse
chain			lie	
doe			load	
dream			meal	
goes				

often	sweet		tall	which
paid			teach	
pie			throat	
snail			toast	
street			weed	

You are playing a word game, and these are your seven tiles. Which two of the words on page 6 could you make with them?

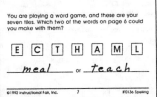

E C T H A M L

meal or teach

©1992 Instructional Fair, Inc.   7   IF0136 Spelling

Brad's Blender

Drop in the right letters and out come perfectly "blended" words! Use the clues to unscramble each group of letters to make a word.

HINT! Each word begins with one of these consonant blends:

bl br cl cr dr fl fr gr pl sl sm st sw gl tr

1. u r t t h (not false) — truth
2. e e s t w (tasting sugary) — sweet
3. d s t u y (to learn) — study
4. a l l m s (not big) — small
5. e e l p s (dream time) — sleep
6. e l n p t y (lots and lots) — plenty
7. g o u p r (a set) — group
8. f o n r t (opposite of back) — front
9. e f l o r w (part of a plant) — flower
10. a c r y z (not dirty or silly) — crazy
11. a e c l n (not dirty) — clean
12. b h r s u (tool for painting) — brush
13. b c k l o (piece of wood) — block
14. d l k n r (to sip liquid) — drink
15. l g d e i (move smoothly) — glide

©1992 Instructional Fair, Inc.   8   IF0136 Spelling

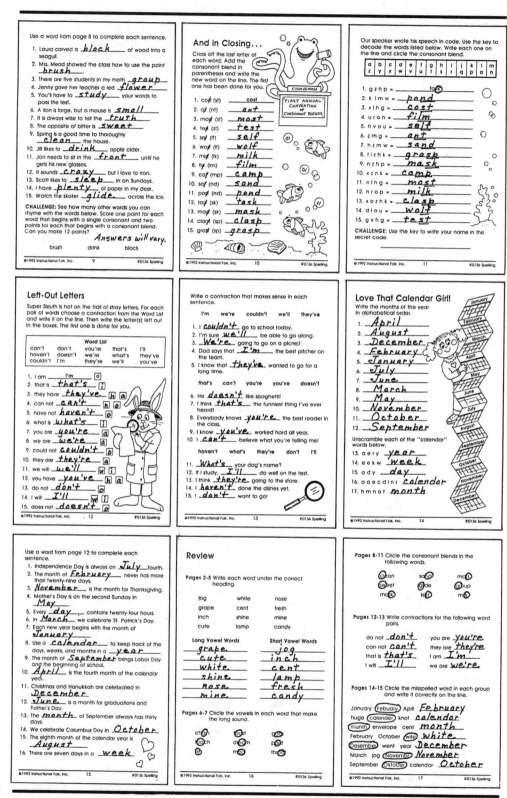

Panel 1 (page 9):

Use a word from page 8 to complete each sentence.

1. Laura carved a **block** of wood into a seagull.
2. Mrs. Mead showed the class how to use the paint **brush**.
3. There are five students in my math **group**.
4. Jenny gave her teacher a red **flower**.
5. You'll have to **study** your words to pass the test.
6. A lion is large, but a mouse is **small**.
7. It is always wise to tell the **truth**.
8. The opposite of bitter is **sweet**.
9. Spring is a good time to thoroughly **clean** the house.
10. Jill likes to **drink** apple cider.
11. Jon needs to sit in the **front** until he gets his new glasses.
12. It sounds **crazy** but I love to iron.
13. Scott likes to **sleep** in on Sundays.
14. I have **plenty** of paper in my desk.
15. Watch the skater **glide** across the ice.

CHALLENGE: See how many other words you can rhyme with the words below. Score one point for each word that begins with a single consonant and two points for each that begins with a consonant blend. Can you make 12 points? **Answers will vary.**

brush   drink   block

©1992 Instructional Fair, Inc.   9   IF0136 Spelling

Panel 2 (page 10): And in Closing...

Cross off the last letter of each word. Add the consonant blend in parentheses and write the new word on the line. The first one has been done for you.

CHAIRMAN
FIRST ANNUAL CONVENTION of CONSONANT BLENDS

1. cop (st) — cost
2. an (nt) — **ant**
3. mos (st) — **most**
4. tes (st) — **test**
5. sel (lf) — **self**
6. wol (lf) — **wolf**
7. mil (lk) — **milk**
8. fil (lm) — **film**
9. cap (mp) — **camp**
10. san (nd) — **sand**
11. pon (nd) — **pond**
12. tas (sk) — **task**
13. mas (sk) — **mask**
14. clas (sp) — **clasp**
15. gras (sp) — **grasp**

©1992 Instructional Fair, Inc.   10   IF0136 Spelling

Panel 3 (page 11):

Our speaker wrote his speech in code. Use the key to decode the words listed below. Write each one on the line and circle the consonant blend.

| a | b | c | d | e | f | g | h | i | j | k | l | m |
|z|y|x|w|v|u|t|s|r|q|p|o|n|

1. gzhp = ta**sk**
2. klmw = **pond**
3. xlhg = **cost**
4. uron = **film**
5. hvou = **self**
6. zmg = **ant**
7. hzmw = **sand**
8. tizhk = **grasp**
9. nzhp = **mask**
10. xznk = **camp**
11. nlhg = **most**
12. nrop = **milk**
13. xozhk = **clasp**
14. dlou = **wolf**
15. gvhg = **test**

CHALLENGE: Use the key to write your name in the secret code.

©1992 Instructional Fair, Inc.   11   IF0136 Spelling

Panel 4 (page 12): Left-Out Letters

Super Sleuth is hot on the trail of stray letters. For each pair of words choose a contraction from the Word List and write it on the line. Then write the letter(s) left out in the boxes. The first one is done for you.

Word List
can't   don't   you're   that's   I'll
haven't   doesn't   we're   what's   they've
couldn't   I'm   they're   we'll   you've

1. I am — **I'm** [a]
2. that is — **that's** [i]
3. they have — **they've** [h a]
4. can not — **can't** [n o]
5. have not — **haven't** [o]
6. what is — **what's** [i]
7. you are — **you're** [a]
8. we are — **we're** [a]
9. could not — **couldn't** [o]
10. they are — **they're** [a]
11. we will — **we'll** [w i]
12. you have — **you've** [h a]
13. do not — **don't** [o]
14. I will — **I'll** [w i]
15. does not — **doesn't** [o]

©1992 Instructional Fair, Inc.   12   IF0136 Spelling

Panel 5 (page 13):

Write a contraction that makes sense in each sentence.

I'm   we're   couldn't   we'll   they've

1. We **couldn't** go to school today.
2. I'm sure **we'll** be able to go along.
3. **We're** going to go on a picnic!
4. Dad says that **I'm** the best pitcher on the team.
5. I know that **they've** wanted to go for a long time.

that's   can't   you're   you've   doesn't

6. He **doesn't** like spaghetti!
7. I think **that's** the funniest thing I've ever heard!
8. Everybody knows **you're** the best reader in the class.
9. I know **you've** worked hard all year.
10. I **can't** believe what you're telling me!

haven't   what's   they're   don't   I'll

11. **What's** your dog's name?
12. If I study, **I'll** do well on the test.
13. I think **they're** going to the store.
14. I **haven't** done the dishes yet.
15. I **don't** want to go!

©1992 Instructional Fair, Inc.   13   IF0136 Spelling

Panel 6 (page 14): Love That Calendar Girl!

Write the months of the year in alphabetical order.

1. **April**
2. **August**
3. **December**
4. **February**
5. **January**
6. **July**
7. **June**
8. **March**
9. **May**
10. **November**
11. **October**
12. **September**

Unscramble each of the "calendar" words below.

13. aery — **year**
14. eekw — **week**
15. ady — **day**
16. aaecdlnr — **calendar**
17. hmnot — **month**

©1992 Instructional Fair, Inc.   14   IF0136 Spelling

Panel 7 (page 15):

Use a word from page 12 to complete each sentence.

1. Independence Day is always on **July** fourth.
2. The month of **February** never has more than twenty-nine days.
3. **November** is the month for Thanksgiving.
4. Mother's Day is on the second Sunday in **May**.
5. Every **day** contains twenty-four hours.
6. In **March** we celebrate St. Patrick's Day.
7. Each new year begins with the month of **January**.
8. Use a **calendar** to keep track of the days, weeks, and months in a **year**.
9. The month of **September** brings Labor Day and the beginning of school.
10. **April** is the fourth month of the calendar year.
11. Christmas and Hanukkah are celebrated in **December**.
12. **June** is a month for graduations and Father's Day.
13. The **month** of September always has thirty days.
14. We celebrate Columbus Day in **October**.
15. The eighth month of the calendar year is **August**.
16. There are seven days in a **week**.

©1992 Instructional Fair, Inc.   15   IF0136 Spelling

Panel 8 (page 16): Review

Pages 2-5 Write each word under the correct heading.

jog   white   nose
grape   cent   fresh
inch   shine   mine
cute   lamp   candy

Long Vowel Words
grape.
cute.
white.
shine.
nose.
mine.

Short Vowel Words
jog
inch
cent
lamp
fresh
candy

Pages 6-7 Circle the vowels in each word that make the long sound.

ch(ai)n   g(oa)t   c(a)ke
t(ea)ch   d(ea)m   p(ai)d
b(ee)   m(ee)n   thr(ee)

©1992 Instructional Fair, Inc.   16   IF0136 Spelling

Panel 9 (page 17):

Pages 8-11 Circle the consonant blends in the following words.

(cl)ean   sc(a)p   mo(nd)
(sw)eet   (gl)ide   (gr)up
ma(sk)   te(st)   mi(lk)

Pages 12-13 Write contractions for the following word pairs.

do not — **don't**   you are — **you're**
can not — **can't**   they are — **they're**
that is — **that's**   I am — **I'm**
I will — **I'll**   we are — **we're**

Pages 14-15 Circle the misspelled word in each group and write it correctly on the line.

January (Febuary) April — **February**
huge (calender) knot — **calendar**
(munth) envelope cent — **month**
February October (wite) — **white**
(Desember) went cent — **December**
March jog (Novembr) — **November**
September (Oktober) calendar — **October**

©1992 Instructional Fair, Inc.   17   IF0136 Spelling

Cheers for the Chief

Use the clues to choose a consonant digraph to complete each word. Then write the word on the line. The first one is done for you.

ch	sh	th	qu	wh

1. not a boo, but a **ch** eer ... cheer
2. not a brave, but the **ch** ief ... **chief**
3. not a minnow, but a **wh** ale ... **whale**
4. not in the light, but in the **sh** adows ... **shadows**
5. not a cape, but a **sh** awl ... **shawl**
6. not a blanket, but a **qu** ilt ... **quilt**
7. not thick, but **th** in ... **thin**
8. not Halloween, but **Th** anksgiving ... **Thanksgiving**
9. not noisy, but **qu** iet ... **quiet**
10. not dull, but **sh** arp ... **sharp**
11. not a crayon, but a piece of **ch** alk ... **chalk**
12. not a 4-leaf clover, but a **sh** amrock ... **shamrock**
13. not keeping, but **sh** aring ... **sharing**
14. not a part, but a **wh** ole ... **whole**
15. not wasteful, but **th** rifty ... **thrifty**

© 1992 Instructional Fair, Inc. 18 IF0136 Spelling

Replace the underlined letter(s) with a consonant digraph that makes a word from page 18.

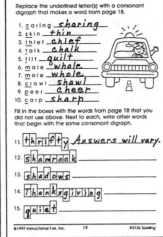

1. c a r ing ... **sharing**
2. s k in ... **thin**
3. t h ief ... **chief**
4. t a lk ... **chalk**
5. t i l t ... **quilt**
6. m a le ... **whale**
7. m o le ... **whole**
8. c r a wl ... **shawl**
9. p e e r ... **cheer**
10. c a r p ... **sharp**

Fill in the boxes with the words from page 18 that you did not use above. Next to each, write other words that begin with the same consonant digraph.

11. t h r i f t y   Answers will vary.
12. s h a m r o c k
13. s h a d o w s
14. T h a n k s g i v i n g
15. q u i e t

© 1992 Instructional Fair, Inc. 19 IF0136 Spelling

Get Wise About Long "Eyes"

Use the clues and the beginning letter(s) in parentheses to make words with the / i / sound. The first one is done for you.

1. airplane ride ... (fl) flight
2. not dim ... (br) **bright**
3. unable to see ... (bl) **blind**
4. opposite of wrong ... (r) **right**
5. not tame ... (w) **wild**
6. pesty black insects ... (fl) **flies**
7. not an adult ... (ch) **child**
8. gentle, kind; not harsh ... (m) **mild**
9. to locate something lost ... (f) **find**
10. make up your ... (m) **mind**
11. opposite of laughs ... (cr) **cries**
12. plural of try ... (tr) **tries**

Add g y to each pair of letters to make a word with the / i / sound. Write the word on the line.

13. s p **y** ... **spy**
14. t r **y** ... **try**
15. w h **y** ... **why**

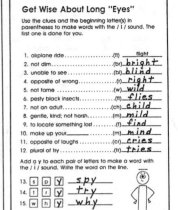

© 1992 Instructional Fair, Inc. 20 IF0136 Spelling

Write words from page 20 that rhyme with each word.

fight	kind
1. **bright**	4. **blind**
2. **flight**	5. **find**
3. **right**	6. **mind**

spies	fly
7. **cries**	10. **spy**
8. **flies**	11. **try**
9. **tries**	12. **why**

Write the words from page 20 that you did not use above.

13. **child**
14. **mild**
15. **wild**

CHALLENGE: Can you think of other words to rhyme with these words? Use a dictionary to check your spelling.

fight	kind	fly

Answers will vary.

© 1992 Instructional Fair, Inc. 21 IF0136 Spelling

The Odd Couples

Write a word from the Word List to complete each puzzle. The first one is done for you.

	Word List		
book	flour	auto	soil	moon
wood	count	because	coin	tooth
foot	mouth	sauce	noise	loose

1. louse – ou + oo = ... **loose**
2. boof – 1 + k = ... **book**
3. soul – ou + ol = ... **soil**
4. spoon – sp + m = ... **moon**
5. nose – o + ol = ... **noise**
6. wool – 1 + d = ... **wood**
7. tool – l + th = ... **tooth**
8. cent – e + ou = ... **count**
9. become – ome + ause = ... **because**
10. floor – oo + ou = ... **flour**
11. fool – l + t = ... **foot**
12. coil – l + n = ... **coin**
13. south – s + m = ... **mouth**
14. Pluto – Pl + a = ... **auto**
15. soot – oot + auce = ... **sauce**

© 1992 Instructional Fair, Inc. 22 IF0136 Spelling

Fill in each blank with a word from page 22.

1. Rebecca planted the seed in a pot of **soil**
2. The button on my coat is **loose.**
3. Another word for **auto** is car.
4. Matt broke his **foot** playing football.
5. Close your **mouth** when chewing food.
6. You use **flour** to make pie dough.
7. Mrs. Bradford had an old, gold **coin** called a doubloon.
8. Brennan lost a front **tooth** in school.
9. Joel looked at the **moon** through his telescope.
10. Dad is chopping **wood** for the fireplace.
11. Meg's favorite **book** is Tuck Everlasting.
12. Michael likes barbeque **sauce** on his hamburger.
13. The car is making a strange **noise.**
14. We should always **count** one's blessings.
15. Rob likes pizza **because** it tastes so good.

© 1992 Instructional Fair, Inc. 23 IF0136 Spelling

Looking for Double Trouble

Double the final consonant of each word in parentheses and add ed or ing so that the sentence makes sense. Write the word on the line.

1. The chocolate (drip) **dripped** all over the ice cream.
2. Amy's cat is (rub) **rubbing** its head against my leg.
3. Bill is (set) **setting** the table.
4. Mother (thin) **thinned** the soup with water.
5. Jason has a (spot) **spotted** dog.
6. Meg (ship) **shipped** a gift to her cousin.
7. The hare (hop) **hopped** across the field.
8. Krista spent the day (shop) **shopping.**
9. Eric made noise (drum) **drumming** his drums.
10. Aaron (slip) **slipped** on a patch of ice.
11. Dad (jog) **jogged** around the block.
12. Our dog (beg) **begged** for a piece of pizza.
13. Is Matt (gab) **gabbing** on the phone?
14. Beth is (sit) **sitting** in the rocking chair.
15. Jenna's favorite sport is (swim) **swimming.**

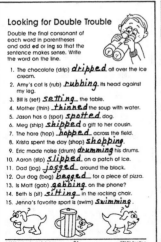

© 1992 Instructional Fair, Inc. 24 IF0136 Spelling

Dividing these words into syllables really isn't difficult. Just separate the words between the double consonants! The first one is done for you.

1. shopping	shop	ping
2. spotted	**spot**	**ted**
3. sitting	**sit**	**ting**
4. drumming	**drum**	**ming**
5. rubbing	**rub**	**bing**
6. swimming	**swim**	**ming**
7. setting	**set**	**ting**
8. gabbing	**gab**	**bing**

Double the final consonant and add ed before writing each word. Circle d if the final sound is the sound of /d/ or t if the final sound is the sound of /t/.

9. drip	**dripped**	d	ⓣ
10. ship	**shipped**	d	ⓣ
11. beg	**begged**	ⓓ	t
12. slip	**slipped**	d	ⓣ
13. thin	**thinned**	ⓓ	t
14. hop	**hopped**	d	ⓣ
15. jog	**jogged**	ⓓ	t

© 1992 Instructional Fair, Inc. 25 IF0136 Spelling

Sh! The Consonants Are Sleeping....

Circle the silent consonant in each word. Write the word in the correct word box.

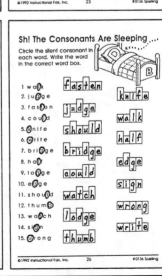

1. w a l k ... **fasten**
2. j u d g e ... **knife**
3. f a s t e n ... **judge**
4. c o u l d ... **walk**
5. w r i t e ... **should**
6. w r i t e ... **half**
7. b r i d g e ... **bridge**
8. h a l f ... **edge**
9. l o d g e ... **could**
10. e d g e ... **sign**
11. s h o u l d ... **watch**
12. t h u m b ... **wrong**
13. w a t c h ... **lodge**
14. s i g n ... **write**
15. w r o n g ... **thumb**

© 1992 Instructional Fair, Inc. 26 IF0136 Spelling

© 1992 Instructional Fair, Inc.   IF0136 Answer Key

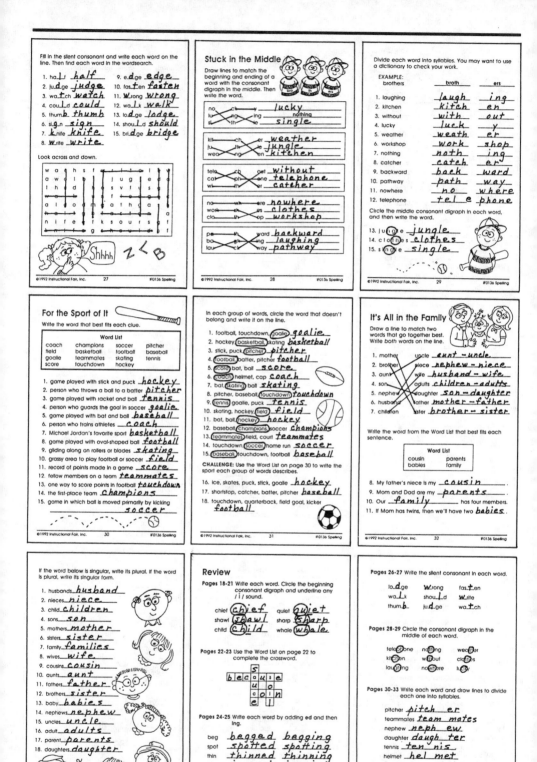

Panel 1 (page 27)

Fill in the silent consonant and write each word on the line. Then find each word in the wordsearch.

1. ha**l**f — _half_
2. ju**d**ge — _judge_
3. wa**t**ch — _watch_
4. cou**l**d — _could_
5. thum**b** — _thumb_
6. si**g**n — _sign_
7. **k**nife — _knife_
8. **w**rite — _write_
9. e**d**ge — _edge_
10. fas**t**en — _fasten_
11. **w**rong — _wrong_
12. wa**l**k — _walk_
13. lo**d**ge — _lodge_
14. shou**l**d — _should_
15. bri**d**ge — _bridge_

Look across and down.

Shhhh Z < B

©1992 Instructional Fair, Inc.   27   IF0136 Spelling

Panel 2 (page 28)

Stuck in the Middle

Draw lines to match the beginning and ending of a word with the consonant digraph in the middle. Then write the word.

lucky
nothing
single

weather
jungle
kitchen

without
telephone
catcher

nowhere
clothes
workshop

backward
laughing
pathway

©1992 Instructional Fair, Inc.   28   IF0136 Spelling

Panel 3 (page 29)

Divide each word into syllables. You may want to use a dictionary to check your work.

EXAMPLE:
brothers   broth   ers

1. laughing	laugh	ing
2. kitchen	kitch	en
3. without	with	out
4. lucky	luck	y
5. weather	weath	er
6. workshop	work	shop
7. nothing	noth	ing
8. catcher	catch	er
9. backward	back	ward
10. pathway	path	way
11. nowhere	no	where
12. telephone	tel e	phone

Circle the middle consonant digraph in each word, and then write the word.

13. ju**ng**le _jungle_
14. clo**th**es _clothes_
15. si**ng**le _single_

©1992 Instructional Fair, Inc.   29   IF0136 Spelling

Panel 4 (page 30)

For the Sport of It

Write the word that best fits each clue.

Word List

coach	champions	soccer	pitcher
field	basketball	football	baseball
goalie	teammates	skating	tennis
score	touchdown	hockey	

1. game played with stick and puck _hockey_
2. person who throws a ball to a batter _pitcher_
3. game played with racket and ball _tennis_
4. person who guards the goal in soccer _goalie_
5. game played with bat and ball _baseball_
6. person who trains athletes _coach_
7. Michael Jordan's favorite sport _basketball_
8. game played with oval-shaped ball _football_
9. gliding along on rollers or blades _skating_
10. grassy area to play football or soccer _field_
11. record of points made in a game _score_
12. fellow members on a team _teammates_
13. one way to score points in football _touchdown_
14. the first-place team _champions_
15. game in which ball is moved primarily by kicking _soccer_

©1992 Instructional Fair, Inc.   30   IF0136 Spelling

Panel 5 (page 31)

In each group of words, circle the word that doesn't belong and write it on the line.

1. football, touchdown, (goalie) _goalie_
2. hockey, (basketball), skating _basketball_
3. stick, puck, (pitcher) _pitcher_
4. (football), batter, pitcher _football_
5. (score), bat, ball _score_
6. (coach), helmet, cap _coach_
7. bat, (skating), ball _skating_
8. pitcher, baseball, (touchdown) _touchdown_
9. (tennis), goalie, puck _tennis_
10. skating, hockey, (field) _field_
11. bat, ball, (hockey) _hockey_
12. baseball, (champions), soccer _champions_
13. (teammates), field, court _teammates_
14. touchdown, (soccer), home run _soccer_
15. (baseball), touchdown, football _baseball_

CHALLENGE: Use the Word List on page 30 to write the sport each group of words describes.

16. ice, skates, puck, stick, goalie _hockey_
17. shortstop, catcher, batter, pitcher _baseball_
18. touchdown, quarterback, field goal, kicker _football_

©1992 Instructional Fair, Inc.   31   IF0136 Spelling

Panel 6 (page 32)

It's All in the Family

Draw a line to match two words that go together best. Write both words on the line.

1. mother — uncle _aunt – uncle_
2. brother — niece _nephew – niece_
3. aunt — wife _husband – wife_
4. son — adults _children – adults_
5. nephew — daughter _son – daughter_
6. husband — father _mother – father_
7. children — sister _brother – sister_

Write the word from the Word List that best fits each sentence.

Word List

| cousin | parents |
| babies | family |

8. My father's niece is my _cousin_
9. Mom and Dad are my _parents_
10. Our _family_ has four members.
11. If Mom has twins, then we'll have two _babies_.

©1992 Instructional Fair, Inc.   32   IF0136 Spelling

Panel 7 (page 33)

If the word below is singular, write its plural. If the word is plural, write its singular form.

1. husbands _husband_
2. nieces _niece_
3. child _children_
4. sons _son_
5. mothers _mother_
6. sisters _sister_
7. family _families_
8. wives _wife_
9. cousins _cousin_
10. aunts _aunt_
11. fathers _father_
12. brothers _sister_
13. baby _babies_
14. nephews _nephew_
15. uncles _uncle_
16. adult _adults_
17. parent _parents_
18. daughters _daughter_

©1992 Instructional Fair, Inc.   33   IF0136 Spelling

Panel 8 (page 34)

Review

Pages 18-21 Write each word. Circle the beginning consonant digraph and underline any / ī / sound.

chief (ch)ie̲f   quiet qu̲i̲e̲t
shawl (sh)aw̲l   sharp (sh)ar̲p
child (ch)i̲l̲d   whale (wh)a̲le̲

Pages 22-23 Use the Word List on page 22 to complete the crossword.

```
    s
b e c a u s e
    u
    c o i n
    e
    l
```

Pages 24-25 Write each word by adding ed and then ing.

beg _begged_ _begging_
spot _spotted_ _spotting_
thin _thinned_ _thinning_
jog _jogged_ _jogging_

©1992 Instructional Fair, Inc.   34   IF0136 Spelling

Panel 9 (page 35)

Pages 26-27 Write the silent consonant in each word.

lo**d**ge   **w**rong   fas**t**en
wa**l**k   shou**l**d   **w**rite
thum**b**   ju**d**ge   wa**t**ch

Pages 28-29 Circle the consonant digraph in the middle of each word.

tele**ph**one   no**th**ing   wea**th**er
ki**tch**en   wi**th**out   clo**th**es
lau**gh**ing   no**wh**ere   lu**ck**y

Pages 30-33 Write each word and draw lines to divide each one into syllables.

pitcher _pitch er_
teammates _team mates_
nephew _neph ew_
daughter _daugh ter_
tennis _ten nis_
helmet _hel met_
parents _par ents_

©1992 Instructional Fair, Inc.   35   IF0136 Spelling

©1992 Instructional Fair, Inc.   IF0136 Answer Key

The Mysterious Code

Super Sleuth is at work on a case. Use his key to decode each word. Use the Word List to check your spelling.

a	b	c	d	e	f	g	h	i	j	k	l	m
z	y	x	w	v	u	t	s	r	q	p	o	n

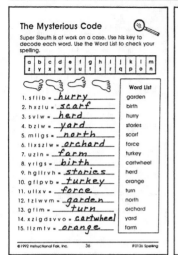

Word List

garden, birth, hurry, stories, scarf, force, turkey, cartwheel, herd, orange, turn, north, orchard, yard, farm

1. sflib = **hurry**
2. hxzlu = **scarf**
3. svlw = **herd**
4. bzlw = **yard**
5. mllgs = **north**
6. llxszlw = **orchard**
7. uzln = **farm**
8. yrlgs = **birth**
9. hgllrvh = **stories**
10. gflpvb = **turkey**
11. ullxv = **force**
12. tzlwvm = **garden**
13. gflm = **turn**
14. xzlgdsvvo = **cartwheel**
15. llzmtv = **orange**

Add ar, er, or or ur to each of these group of letters to make a word from page 36.

1. st**or**ies
2. y**ar**d
3. c**ar**twheel
4. **or**chard
5. h**ur**ry
6. f**or**ce
7. h**er**d
8. g**ar**den
9. t**ur**n
10. n**or**th
11. t**ur**key
12. **or**ange
13. f**ar**m
14. b**ir**th
15. sc**ar**f

Write five words from above that have the /ûr/ sound as in turn.

hurry   turn   birth
herd   turkey

Write five words from above that have the /ôr/ sound as in horse.

stories   force   orange
orchard   north

Write five words from above that have the /är/ sound as in hard.

yard   garden   scarf
cartwheel   farm

CHALLENGE: Use the key on page 36 to write your name in the secret code.

_____

One Man's Ceiling Is His Neighbor's Floor

Write each ei word below the sound it makes.

Word List

neighbor, receive, receipt, rein, veil, eight, ceiling, protein

/ā/	/ē/
neighbor	receive
rein	receipt
veil	ceiling
eight	protein

Write each word beside the sound its underlined vowel makes.

Word List

sprayer, people, party, gray, usually, clay

/ā/	sprayer gray clay
/ē/	people party usually

Use the words from page 40 to match these phonetic spellings.

1. /sē´ ling/ **ceiling**
2. /grā/ **gray**
3. /āt/ **eight**
4. /yōō´ zhōō ə lē/ **usually**
5. /pē´ pəl/ **people**
6. /nā´ bər/ **neighbor**
7. /ri sēt´/ **receipt**
8. /klā/ **clay**
9. /rān/ **rein**
10. /pär´ tē/ **party**
11. /ri sēv´/ **receive**
12. /vāl/ **veil**
13. /prō´ tēn/ **protein**
14. /sprā´ ər/ **sprayer**

CHALLENGE: The ei in neither and either can be pronounced with a /ē/ or /ī/ sound. Use a dictionary to write both phonetic spellings of each word.

15. either **ē´thər   ī´thər**
16. neither **nē´thər   nī´thər**

It "Bears" Repeating

You may want to use a dictionary to help you write the correct word after each definition.

bear	large, hairy mammal	**bear**
bare	without fur or hair	**bare**
their	In that place	**there**
they're	belonging to them	**their**
there	they are	**they're**
pear	two matched objects	**pair**
pair	to peel or remove skin or rind	**pare**
pare	a fruit that grows on trees	**pear**
hour	belonging to us	**our**
our	a unit of time	**hour**
see	to look	**see**
sea	a body of water	**sea**
to	one more than one	**two**
two	in the direction of	**to**
too	also, or more than enough	**too**

In each set of parentheses, cross out the spelling that is not correct.

Once upon a time, (they/~~their~~) was a (~~pair~~/pair) of (bears/~~bares~~) who decided to go jogging. Actually (~~they~~/there) were three (bears/~~bares~~), but one didn't have a clean sweat suit to wear, so he stayed home.

Anyway, these (~~two~~/too) (bears/~~bares~~) thought they'd go out for (~~they're~~/their) morning jog while (their/~~they're~~) oatmeal cooled, and the other (bear/~~bare~~) was left to (~~pair~~/pare) the apples. One (~~bare~~/bear) thought they should jog along the (sea/~~see~~), but the other thought this would take (~~two~~/too) long, for surely if they were gone more than an (hour/~~our~~), (their/~~they're~~) oatmeal would get (~~two~~/too) cold.

They finally decided to follow the path that goes past a farmer's old (pear/~~pair~~) tree where they could (see/~~sea~~) him working. As they jogged by, the first (bear/~~bare~~) shouted, "Why don't you stop by (~~hour~~/our) place in an (hour/~~our~~) or (~~two~~/too), to (see/~~sea~~) the videos of (our/~~hour~~) vacation?"

They were home in less than an (~~our~~/hour). By the time the farmer arrived, they had finished (~~they're~~/their) breakfast and were ready (~~two~~/to) spend the rest of the morning showing (their/~~there~~) vacation videos to (~~two~~/too) (~~they're~~/their) delightful neighbor.

Decisions; Decisions

Add ed or ing to each word in parentheses, and write the word on the line.

1. Beth (enjoy) **enjoyed** the art fair.
2. Kara is (stay) **staying** with friends.
3. Miss Scott's class (play) **played** Twenty Questions.
4. Grandpa is (buy) **buying** a new car.
5. Kurt is (study) **studying** his math.
6. Mr. Cole is (carry) **carrying** his coat.

Change the y to i and add ed to each word in parentheses. Write the word on the line.

7. Kelly (worry) **worried** that she wouldn't finish in time.
8. Mom (fry) **fried** some bacon for our breakfast.

Drop the silent e and add ed or ing to each word in parentheses. Write the word on the line.

9. Jennie is (care) **caring** for the baby.
10. Katie (change) **changed** clothes.
11. The boys are (have) **having** a good time at the park.
12. Dad is (leave) **leaving** for London.
13. George (vote) **voted** for himself.
14. Michelle is (shake) **shaking** the package.
15. Adam (separate) **separated** the eggs to make an omelet.

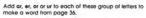

Circle the misspelled word in each row and write it correctly on the line.

1. caring, ~~worryed~~, changed **worried**
2. ~~haveing~~, voted, staying **having**
3. voted, caring, ~~playyed~~ **played**
4. ~~carying~~, separated, enjoyed **carrying**
5. buying, played, ~~fryed~~ **fried**
6. changed, ~~voteed~~, leaving **voted**
7. studying, ~~shakeing~~, staying **shaking**
8. played, fried, ~~studdying~~ **studying**
9. ~~staiing~~, having, shaking **staying**
10. carrying, ~~careing~~, changed **caring**
11. having, studying, ~~enjoied~~ **enjoyed**
12. fried, ~~leaveing~~, caring **leaving**
13. ~~seperated~~, carrying, voted **separated**
14. ~~changged~~, shaking, staying **changed**
15. leaving, worried, ~~buing~~ **buying**

Do W's Trouble You?

Add aw to complete each word in the first box, ew, the words in the second box, and ow, the words in the third box. Then write each word on the line below it. The first one has been done for you.

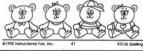

aw		
shawl / **shawl**	straw / **straw**	crawl / **crawl**
hawk / **hawk**	gnaw / **gnaw**	draw / **draw**

ew		
view / **view**	crew / **crew**	threw / **threw**
new / **new**	blew / **blew**	few / **few**

ow		
plow / **plow**	allow / **allow**	shower / **shower**
towel / **towel**	frown / **frown**	power / **power**

IF0136 Answer Key

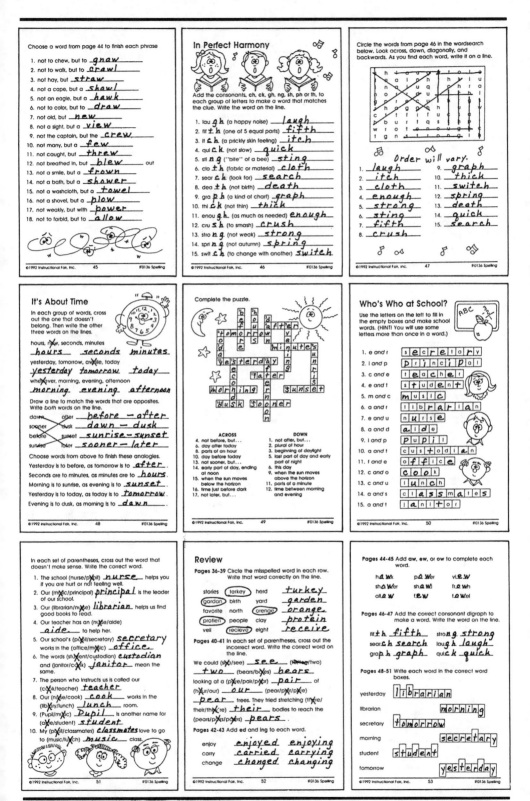

Choose a word from page 44 to finish each phrase

1. not to chew, but to **gnaw**
2. not to walk, but to **crawl**
3. not hay, but **straw**
4. not a cape, but a **shawl**
5. not an eagle, but a **hawk**
6. not to color, but to **draw**
7. not old, but **new**
8. not a sight, but a **view**
9. not the captain, but the **crew**
10. not many, but a **few**
11. not caught, but **threw**
12. not breathed in, but **blew** out
13. not a smile, but a **frown**
14. not a bath, but a **shower**
15. not a washcloth, but a **towel**
16. not a shovel, but a **plow**
17. not weakly, but with **power**
18. not to forbid, but to **allow**

©1992 Instructional Fair, Inc. 45 IF0136 Spelling

In Perfect Harmony

Add the consonants, ch, ck, gh, gh, ng, sh, ph or th, to each group of letters to make a word that matches the clue. Write the word on the line.

1. lau **gh** (a happy noise) **laugh**
2. fil **th** (one of 5 equal parts) **fifth**
3. it **ch** (a prickly skin feeling) **itch**
4. qui **ck** (not slow) **quick**
5. sti **ng** ("bite" of a bee) **sting**
6. clo **th** (fabric or material) **cloth**
7. sear **ch** (look for) **search**
8. dea **th** (not birth) **death**
9. gra **ph** (a kind of chart) **graph**
10. thi **ck** (not thin) **thick**
11. enou **gh** (as much as needed) **enough**
12. cru **sh** (to smash) **crush**
13. stro **ng** (not weak) **strong**
14. spri **ng** (not autumn) **spring**
15. swit **ch** (to change with another) **switch**

©1992 Instructional Fair, Inc. 46 IF0136 Spelling

Circle the words from page 46 in the wordsearch below. Look across, down, diagonally, and backwards. As you find each word, write it on a line.

Order will vary.

1. **laugh**   9. **graph**
2. **itch**   10. **thick**
3. **cloth**   11. **switch**
4. **enough**   12. **spring**
5. **strong**   13. **death**
6. **sting**   14. **quick**
7. **fifth**   15. **search**
8. **crush**

©1992 Instructional Fair, Inc. 47 IF0136 Spelling

It's About Time

In each group of words, cross out the one that doesn't belong. Then write the other three words on the lines.

hours, now, seconds, minutes
hours   seconds   minutes

yesterday, tomorrow, awhile, today
yesterday   tomorrow   today

whenever, morning, evening, afternoon
morning   evening   afternoon

Draw a line to match the words that are opposites. Write both words on the line.

dawn — after → **before — after**
sooner — dusk → **dawn — dusk**
before — sunset → **sunrise — sunset**
sunrise — later → **sooner — later**

Choose words from above to finish these analogies.

Yesterday is to before, as tomorrow is to **after**
Seconds are to minutes, as minutes are to **hours**
Morning is to sunrise, as evening is to **sunset**
Yesterday is to today, as today is to **tomorrow**
Evening is to dusk, as morning is to **dawn**

©1992 Instructional Fair, Inc. 48 IF0136 Spelling

Complete the puzzle.

ACROSS
4. not before, but...
6. day after today
8. parts of an hour
10. day before today
13. not sooner, but...
14. early part of day, ending at noon
15. when the sun moves below the horizon
16. time just before dark
17. not later, but...

DOWN
1. not after, but...
2. plural of hour
3. beginning of daylight
5. last part of day and early part of night
6. this day
9. when the sun moves above the horizon
11. parts of a minute
12. time between morning and evening

©1992 Instructional Fair, Inc. 49 IF0136 Spelling

Who's Who at School?

Use the letters on the left to fill in the empty boxes and make school words. (HINT! You will use some letters more than once in a word.)

1. e and r — s e c r e t a r y
2. i and p — p r i n c i p a l
3. c and e — t e a c h e r
4. e and t — s t u d e n t
5. m and c — m u s i c
6. a and r — l i b r a r i a n
7. e and u — n u r s e
8. a and d — a i d e
9. i and p — p u p i l
10. a and t — c u s t o d i a n
11. f and e — o f f i c e
12. c and o — c o o k
13. c and u — l u n c h
14. a and s — c l a s s m a t e s
15. a and t — j a n i t o r

©1992 Instructional Fair, Inc. 50 IF0136 Spelling

In each set of parentheses, cross out the word that doesn't make sense. Write the correct word.

1. The school (nurse/pupil) **nurse** helps you if you are hurt or not feeling well.
2. Our (music/principal) **principal** is the leader of our school.
3. Our (librarian/nurse) **librarian** helps us find good books to read.
4. Our teacher has an (nurse/aide) **aide** to help her.
5. Our school's (pupil/secretary) **secretary** works in the (office/music) **office**.
6. The words (student/custodian) **custodian** and (janitor/cook) **janitor** mean the same.
7. The person who instructs us is called our (cook/teacher) **teacher**.
8. Our (nurse/cook) **cook** works in the (library/lunch) **lunch** room.
9. (Pupil/music) **Pupil** is another name for (aide/student) **student**.
10. My (pupil/classmates) **classmates** love to go to (music/lunch) **music** class.

©1992 Instructional Fair, Inc. 51 IF0136 Spelling

Review

Pages 36-39 Circle the misspelled word in each row. Write that word correctly on the line.

stories (turkey) herd — **turkey**
(gardan) birth yard — **garden**
favorite north (orenge) — **orange**
(protien) people clay — **protein**
veil (recieve) eight — **receive**

Pages 40-41 In each set of parentheses, cross out the incorrect word. Write the correct word on the line.

We could (sea/see) **see** (to/two) **two** (bears/bares) **bears** looking at a (pare/pair/pear) **pair** of (hour/our) **our** (pear/pair/pare) **pear** trees. They tried stretching (there/their/they're) **their** bodies to reach the (pears/pairs/pares) **pears**.

Pages 42-43 Add ed and ing to each word.

enjoy — **enjoyed   enjoying**
carry — **carried   carrying**
change — **changed   changing**

©1992 Instructional Fair, Inc. 52 IF0136 Spelling

Pages 44-45 Add aw, ew, or ow to complete each word.

ha **w** k   p **o** wer   vi **ew**
sh **o** wer   sh **a** wl   fr **o** wn
all **o** w   f **ew**   t **o** wel

Pages 46-47 Add the correct consonant digraph to make a word. Write the word on the line.

fil **th** **fifth**   stro **ng** **strong**
sear **ch** **search**   lau **gh** **laugh**
gra **ph** **graph**   qui **ck** **quick**

Pages 48-51 Write each word in the correct word boxes.

yesterday
librarian — l i b r a r i a n
secretary
morning — m o r n i n g
student
tomorrow — t o m o r r o w

(secretary) — s e c r e t a r y
(student) — s t u d e n t
(yesterday) — y e s t e r d a y

©1992 Instructional Fair, Inc. 53 IF0136 Spelling

IF0136 Answer Key

Buried Treasure

Unscramble the letters to form words from the Word List.

1. a e e l p s — **please**
2. c d l o s — **scold**
3. a e c m r s — **scream**
4. a f l o t — **float**
5. d l h o — **hold**
6. b e f i r — **brief**
7. w o n k — **know**
8. a d o r — **road**
9. n o s w — **snow**
10. d g l o — **gold**
11. l e e c p — **piece**
12. e i f h t — **thief**
13. a e h t w — **wheat**
14. o a s t t — **toast**
15. l o d f — **fold**

		Word List		
piece	gold	fold	scream	float
brief	hold	know	wheat	road
thief	scold	snow	please	toast

©1992 Instructional Fair, Inc.　54　IF0136 Spelling

Use the words from page 54 to finish these analogies.

1. Beans are to peas, as oats are to **wheat**
2. Summer is to rain, as winter is to **snow**
3. Kept is to keep, as held is to **hold**
4. Grass is to yard, as pavement is to **road**
5. Down is to up, as sink is to **float**
6. Quiet is to whisper, as loud is to **scream**
7. Ruby is to diamond, as silver is to **gold**
8. Wrinkle is to crinkle, as crease is to **fold**
9. Long is to lengthy, as short is to **brief**
10. Right is to praise, as wrong is to **scold**
11. Egg is to fry, as bread is to **toast**
12. Total is to whole, as part is to **piece**
13. Find is to policeman, as steal is to **thief**
14. Grew is to grow, as knew is to **know**
15. Frown is to displease, as smile is to **please**

©1992 Instructional Fair, Inc.　55　IF0136 Spelling

Compound Nouns

Read each clue and pay close attention to the underlined words. Write a compound word that the clue describes.

1. a <u>rope</u> you <u>jump</u> over — **jumprope**
2. a <u>ball</u> of <u>snow</u> — **snowball**
3. <u>corn</u> that will <u>pop</u> — **popcorn**
4. the <u>day</u> of <u>birth</u> — **birthday**
5. a <u>bow</u> of colors in the sky after a <u>rain</u> — **rainbow**
6. a <u>paper</u> with <u>news</u> — **newspaper**
7. the <u>end</u> of the <u>week</u> — **weekend**
8. when <u>hair</u> is <u>cut</u> — **haircut**
9. <u>ground</u> to <u>play</u> on — **playground**
10. mechanical <u>writer</u> to <u>type</u> with — **typewriter**
11. a <u>nut</u> the size of a <u>pea</u> — **peanut**
12. a <u>flake</u> of <u>snow</u> — **snowflake**
13. a <u>shell</u> by the <u>sea</u> — **seashell**
14. a <u>deer</u> that can be harnessed and guided with <u>reins</u> — **reindeer**

sea + shell = seashell

©1992 Instructional Fair, Inc.　56　IF0136 Spelling

In each section write the letter to match the two words of each compound word. Write the compound word and then write the number of syllables in that word in the box.

snow	_a_	a. deer	**snowball**	2
rein	_a_	b. paper	**reindeer**	2
play	_d_	c. day	**playground**	2
sea	_f_	d. ground	**seashell**	2
news	_b_	e. nut	**newspaper**	3
birth	_c_	f. shell	**birthday**	2
pea	_e_	g. ball	**peanut**	2

week	_d_	a. flake	**weekend**	2
snow	_a_	b. bow	**snowflake**	2
hair	_e_	c. corn	**haircut**	2
rain	_b_	d. end	**rainbow**	2
jump	_f_	e. cut	**jumprope**	2
type	_g_	f. rope	**typewriter**	3
pop	_c_	g. writer	**popcorn**	2

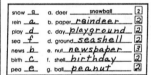

sea + horse = seahorse

©1992 Instructional Fair, Inc.　57　IF0136 Spelling

Perplexed by Plurals?

Most nouns are made plural by just adding s.

Examples: girl, girls　boy, boys

Words that end in s, x, ch or sh, add es. Write the plural for each of these nouns.

1. dish — **dishes**
2. gas — **gases**
3. brush — **brushes**
4. tax — **taxes**
5. box — **boxes**
6. match — **matches**
7. boss — **bosses**
8. sandwich — **sandwiches**

Words that end in y, preceded by a consonant, change the y to an i before adding es. Write the plural for each of these nouns.

9. country — **countries**
10. party — **parties**
11. lady — **ladies**
12. glossary — **glossaries**

Some words that end in f (or fe), change the f (or fe) to v before adding es. Write the plural for each of these nouns.

13. knife — **knives**
14. elf — **elves**
15. wife — **wives**
16. half — **halves**

©1992 Instructional Fair, Inc.　58　IF0136 Spelling

Fill in each blank with the plural form of a word from the Word Box.

box	sandwich	half	glossary

1. Mom cut the orange into two **halves**
2. Meg and Laura made **sandwiches** for the picnic.
3. Many non-fiction books have **glossaries**
4. We packed our dishes in **boxes**

match	lady	knife	brush

5. The **ladies** rode to work together.
6. The **knives** go next to the spoons.
7. Dad needs **matches** to start the campfire.
8. The painter used several different **brushes**

tax	wife	boss	party

9. The men's **wives** went sailing.
10. I was invited to two **parties** last night.
11. On April 15th, everyone pays their **taxes**
12. The **bosses** gave Julie flowers on Secretaries' Day.

dish	country	gas	elf

13. Helium and oxygen are both **gases**
14. Dad washed the **dishes** while I dried them.
15. The **elves** made shoes for the cobbler.
16. Our trip took us through two **countries**

©1992 Instructional Fair, Inc.　59　IF0136 Spelling

Double Your Pleasure

Complete each word by adding double consonants. Then write the word.

1. h a m m e r (a tool) — **hammer**
2. d e s s e r t (after dinner sweets) — **dessert**
3. b a l l o o n (a party decoration) — **balloon**
4. s u p p e r (evening meal) — **supper**
5. b l i z z a r d (bad snowstorm) — **blizzard**
6. w i n n e r (not the loser) — **winner**
7. s u m m e r (not winter) — **summer**
8. s o r r y (feeling regret) — **sorry**
9. j u g g l e (a clown's trick) — **juggle**
10. f o g g y (cloudlike mist) — **foggy**
11. v a l l e y (between mountains) — **valley**
12. l e t t e r (a note) — **letter**
13. l e s s o n (something taught) — **lesson**
14. b o t t o m (not top) — **bottom**
15. c o t t o n (a natural fabric) — **cotton**

©1992 Instructional Fair, Inc.　60　IF0136 Spelling

Divide each word between the double consonant and write it on the lines. The first one has been done for you.

1. blizzard	**bliz**	**zard**
2. juggle	**jug**	**gle**
3. cotton	**cot**	**ton**
4. hammer	**ham**	**mer**
5. lesson	**les**	**son**
6. winner	**win**	**ner**
7. balloon	**bal**	**loon**
8. valley	**val**	**ley**
9. supper	**sup**	**per**
10. bottom	**bot**	**tom**
11. letter	**let**	**ter**
12. sorry	**sor**	**ry**
13. dessert	**des**	**sert**
14. foggy	**fog**	**gy**
15. summer	**sum**	**mer**

HINT! Do you get confused between dessert and desert? Look at the ss in dessert and think that two desserts might be just fine. Then look at the s in desert and think that one desert is more than enough for anybody!

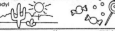

©1992 Instructional Fair, Inc.　61　IF0136 Spelling

Before and After

A prefix is a syllable placed in front of a base word.

Examples: a-, dis-, re-, mis-

A suffix is a letter or syllable added to the end of a base word.

Examples: -ly, -ful, -y, -able, -ed

Decide if each word in the Word List has a prefix or a suffix. Write it under the correct heading.

	Word List	
apart	mistake	discover	rewrite
closely	difficulty	personally	comfortable
healthy	around	answered	dishonest
rebuild	suddenly	misspell	forgetful

Words with Prefixes	Words with Suffixes
apart	closely
rebuild	healthy
mistake	difficulty
around	suddenly
discover	personally
misspell	answered
rewrite	comfortable
dishonest	forgetful

©1992 Instructional Fair, Inc.　62　IF0136 Spelling

IF0136 Answer Key

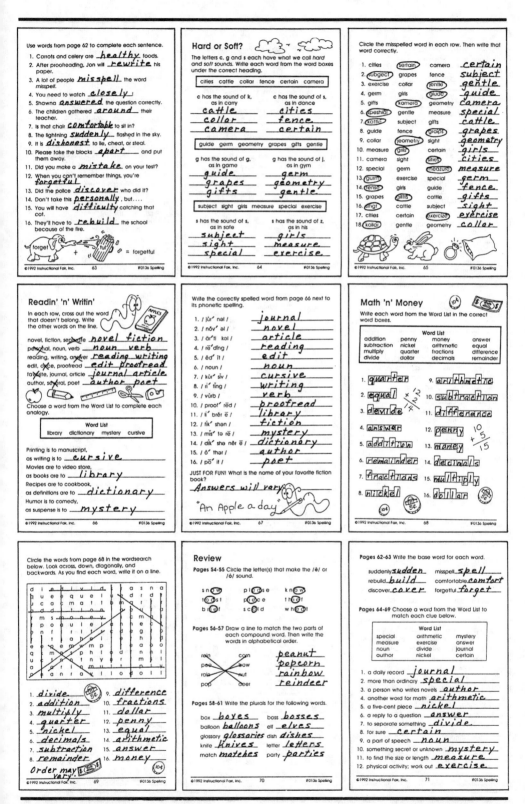

Panel 1 (page 63):

Use words from page 62 to complete each sentence.

1. Carrots and celery are **healthy** foods.
2. After proofreading, Jon will **rewrite** his paper.
3. A lot of people **misspell** the word misspell.
4. You need to listen **closely**.
5. Shawna **answered** the question correctly.
6. The children gathered **around** their teacher.
7. Is that chair **comfortable** to sit in?
8. The lightning **suddenly** flashed in the sky.
9. It is **dishonest** to lie, cheat, or steal.
10. Please take the blocks **apart** and put them away.
11. Did you make a **mistake** on your test?
12. When you can't remember things, you're **forgetful**.
13. Did the police **discover** who did it?
14. Don't take this **personally**, but....
15. You will have **difficulty** catching that cat.
16. They'll have to **rebuild** the school because of the fire.

forget ✗ ○ = forgetful

©1992 Instructional Fair, Inc.   63   IF0136 Spelling

Panel 2 (page 64): Hard or Soft?

The letters c, g and s each have what we call hard and soft sounds. Write each word from the word boxes under the correct heading.

cities cattle collar fence certain camera

c has the sound of k, as in carry	c has the sound of s, as in dance
cattle	cities
collar	fence
camera	certain

guide germ geometry grapes gifts gentle

g has the sound of g, as in game	g has the sound of j, as in gym
guide	germ
grapes	geometry
gifts	gentle

subject sight girls measure special exercise

s has the sound of s, as in safe	s has the sound of z, as in his
subject	girls
sight	measure
special	exercise

©1992 Instructional Fair, Inc.   64   IF0136 Spelling

Panel 3 (page 65):

Circle the misspelled word in each row. Then write that word correctly.

1. cities / (certain) / camera — certain
2. (subject) / grapes / fence — subject
3. exercise / collar / (gentle) — gentle
4. germ / girls / (guide) — guide
5. gifts / (kamera) / geometry — camera
6. (speshial) / gentle / measure — special
7. (cattle) / subject / gifts — cattle
8. guide / fence / (graps) — grapes
9. collar / (geometry) / sight — geometry
10. measure / (girls) / certain — girls
11. camera / sight / (sities) — cities
12. special / germ / (meazure) — measure
13. (gurm) / exercise / special — germ
14. (fense) / girls / guide — fence
15. grapes / (gifts) / cattle — gifts
16. (sight) / cattle / subject — sight
17. cities / certain / (exercize) — exercise
18. (kollar) / gentle / geometry — collar

©1992 Instructional Fair, Inc.   65   IF0136 Spelling

Panel 4 (page 66): Readin' 'n' Writin'

In each row, cross out the word that doesn't belong. Write the other words on the line.

novel, fiction, ~~separate~~ — **novel fiction**
~~personal~~, noun, verb — **noun verb**
reading, writing, ~~answer~~ — **reading writing**
edit, ~~once~~, proofread — **edit proofread**
~~fabricate~~, journal, article — **journal article**
author, ~~several~~, poet — **author poet**

Choose a word from the Word List to complete each analogy.

Word List
library dictionary mystery cursive

Printing is to manuscript, as writing is to **cursive**.
Movies are to video store, as books are to **library**.
Recipes are to cookbook, as definitions are to **dictionary**.
Humor is to comedy, as suspense is to **mystery**.

©1992 Instructional Fair, Inc.   66   IF0136 Spelling

Panel 5 (page 67):

Write the correctly spelled word from page 66 next to its phonetic spelling.

1. / jûr′ nəl / — **journal**
2. / nŏv′ əl / — **novel**
3. / är′ ti kəl / — **article**
4. / rē′ dĭng / — **reading**
5. / ĕd′ ĭt / — **edit**
6. / noun / — **noun**
7. / kûr′ sĭv / — **cursive**
8. / rī′ tĭng / — **writing**
9. / vûrb / — **verb**
10. / proof′ rēd / — **proofread**
11. / lī′ brĕr ē / — **library**
12. / fĭk′ shən / — **fiction**
13. / mĭs′ tə rē / — **mystery**
14. / dĭk′ shə nĕr ē / — **dictionary**
15. / ô′ thər / — **author**
16. / pō′ ĭt / — **poet**

JUST FOR FUN! What is the name of your favorite fiction book? **Answers will vary.**

"An Apple a day"

©1992 Instructional Fair, Inc.   67   IF0136 Spelling

Panel 6 (page 68): Math 'n' Money

Write each word from the Word List in the correct word boxes.

Word List
addition penny money answer
subtraction nickel arithmetic equal
multiply quarter fractions difference
divide dollar decimals remainder

1. **quarter**
2. **equal**
3. **divide**
4. **answer**
5. **addition**
6. **remainder**
7. **fractions**
8. **nickel**
9. **arithmetic**
10. **subtraction**
11. **difference**
12. **penny**
13. **money**
14. **decimals**
15. **multiply**
16. **dollar**

©1992 Instructional Fair, Inc.   68   IF0136 Spelling

Panel 7 (page 69):

Circle the words from page 68 in the wordsearch below. Look across, down, diagonally, and backwards. As you find each word, write it on a line.

1. **divide**
2. **addition**
3. **multiply**
4. **quarter**
5. **nickel**
6. **decimals**
7. **subtraction**
8. **remainder**
9. **difference**
10. **fractions**
11. **dollar**
12. **penny**
13. **equal**
14. **arithmetic**
15. **answer**
16. **money**

Order may vary.

©1992 Instructional Fair, Inc.   69   IF0136 Spelling

Panel 8 (page 70): Review

Pages 54-55 Circle the letter(s) that make the /ē/ or /ō/ sound.

sn(ow) pl(ea)se kn(ow)
to(a)st pr(i)nce th(ie)f
br(ie)f sc(o)ld wh(ea)t

Pages 56-57 Draw a line to match the two parts of each compound word. Then write the words in alphabetical order.

rain — corn
pea — bow
rain — nut
pop — deer

peanut
popcorn
rainbow
reindeer

Pages 58-61 Write the plurals for the following words.

box **boxes**   boss **bosses**
balloon **balloons**   elf **elves**
glossary **glossaries** dish **dishes**
knife **knives**   letter **letters**
match **matches**   party **parties**

©1992 Instructional Fair, Inc.   70   IF0136 Spelling

Panel 9 (page 71):

Pages 62-63 Write the base word for each word.

suddenly **sudden**   misspell **spell**
rebuild **build**   comfortable **comfort**
discover **cover**   forgetful **forget**

Pages 64-69 Choose a word from the Word List to match each clue below.

Word List
special arithmetic mystery
measure exercise answer
noun divide journal
author nickel certain

1. a daily record — **journal**
2. more than ordinary — **special**
3. a person who writes novels — **author**
4. another word for math — **arithmetic**
5. a five-cent piece — **nickel**
6. a reply to a question — **answer**
7. to separate something — **divide**
8. for sure — **certain**
9. a part of speech — **noun**
10. something secret or unknown — **mystery**
11. to find the size or length — **measure**
12. physical activity; work out — **exercise**

©1992 Instructional Fair, Inc.   71   IF0136 Spelling

©1992 Instructional Fair, Inc.   IF0136 Answer Key

Add **ar, er, or** or **ur** to each of these group of letters to make a word from page 36.

1. st____ies
2. y____d
3. c____twheel
4. ____chard
5. h____ry

6. f____ce
7. h____d
8. g____den
9. t____n
10. n____th

11. t____key
12. ____ange
13. f____m
14. b____th
15. sc____f

Write five words from above that have the /ûr/ sound as in *heard*.

_____   _____

_____   _____

Write five words from above that have the /ôr/ sound as in *horse*.

_____   _____

_____   _____

Write five words from above that have the /är/ sound as in *hard*.

_____   _____

_____   _____

CHALLENGE: Use the key on page 36 to write your name in the secret code.

_____

One Man's Ceiling Is His Neighbor's Floor

Write each **ei** word below the sound it makes.

Word List		
neighbor	rein	eight
receive	veil	protein
receipt	ceiling	

/ ā /   / ē /

_____   _____

_____   _____

_____   _____

_____   _____

Write each word beside the sound its underlined vowel makes.

Word List		
spr<u>a</u>yer	part<u>y</u>	usuall<u>y</u>
p<u>e</u>ople	gr<u>a</u>y	cl<u>a</u>y

/ ā /   _____ _____ _____

/ ē /   _____ _____ _____

Use the words from page 40 to match these phonetic spellings.

1. / sē´ lǐng / _____

2. / grā / _____

3. / āt / _____

4. / yōō´ zhōō əl ē / _____

5. / pē´ pəl / _____

6. / nā´ bər / _____

7. / rǐ sēt´ / _____

8. / klā / _____

9. / rān / _____

10. / pär´ tē / _____

11. / rǐ sēv´ / _____

12. / vāl / _____

13. / prō´ tēn / _____

14. / sprā´ ər / _____

CHALLENGE: The **ei** in *neither* and *either* can be pronounced with a /ē/ or /ī/ sound. Use a dictionary to write both phonetic spellings of each word.

15. either _____ _____

16. neither _____ _____

It "Bears" Repeating

You may want to use a
dictionary to help you write
the correct word after each
definition.

bear   large, hairy mammal _____

bare   without fur or hair _____

their   in that place _____

they're   belonging to them _____

there   they are _____

pear   two matched objects _____

pair   to peel or remove skin or rind _____

pare   a fruit that grows on trees _____

hour   belonging to us _____

our   a unit of time _____

see   to look _____

sea   a body of water _____

to   one more than one _____

two   in the direction of _____

too   also, or more than enough _____

In each set of parentheses, cross out the spelling that is not correct.

Once upon a time, (their/there) was a (pair/pear) of (bears/bares) who decided to go jogging. Actually (their/there) were three (bears/bares), but one didn't have a clean sweat suit to wear, so he stayed home.

Anyway, these (to/two) (bears/bares) thought they'd go out for (they're/their) morning jog while (their/there) oatmeal cooled, and the other (bear/bare) was left to (pear/pare) the apples. One (bare/bear) thought they should jog along the (sea/see), but the other thought this would take (to/too) long, for surely if they were gone more than an (hour/our), (their/they're) oatmeal would get (to/too) cold.

They finally decided to follow the path that goes past a farmer's old (pear/pare) tree where they could (sea/see) him working. As they jogged by, the first (bear/bare) shouted, "Why don't you stop by (hour/our) place in an (hour/our) or (too/two), to (see/sea) the videos of (our/hour) vacation?"

They were home in less than an (our/hour). By the time the farmer arrived, they had finished (they're/their) breakfast and were ready (two/to) spend the rest of the morning showing (their/there) vacation videos (to/two) (they're/their) delightful neighbor.

Decisions; Decisions

Add **ed** or **ing** to each word in parentheses, and write the word on the line.

1. Beth (enjoy) _____ the art fair.
2. Kara is (stay) _____ with friends.
3. Miss Scott's class (play) _____ *Twenty Questions*.
4. Grandpa is (buy) _____ a new car.
5. Kurt is (study) _____ his math.
6. Mr. Cole is (carry) _____ his coat.

Change the **y** to **i** and add **ed** to each word in parentheses. Write the word on the line.

7. Kelly (worry) _____ that she wouldn't finish in time.
8. Mom (fry) _____ some bacon for our breakfast.

Drop the silent **e** and add **ed** or **ing** to each word in parentheses. Write the word on the line.

9. Jennie is (care) _____ for the baby.
10. Katie (change) _____ clothes.
11. The boys are (have) _____ a good time at the park.
12. Dad is (leave) _____ for London.
13. George (vote) _____ for himself.
14. Michelle is (shake) _____ the package.
15. Adam (separate) _____ the eggs to make an omelet.

Circle the misspelled word in each row and write it correctly on the line.

1. caring, worryed, changed _____

2. haveing, voted, staying _____

3. voted, caring, playyed _____

4. carying, separated, enjoyed _____

5. buying, played, fryed _____

6. changed, voteed, leaving _____

7. studying, shakking, staying _____

8. played, fried, studdying _____

9. staiing, having, shaking _____

10. carrying, careing, changed _____

11. having, studying, enjoied _____

12. fried, leavving, caring _____

13. seperated, carrying, voted _____

14. changged, shaking, staying _____

15. leaving, worried, bying _____

Do W's Trouble You?

Add **aw** to complete each word in the first box, **ew**, the words in the second box, and **ow**, the words in the third box. Then write each word on the line below it. the first one has been done for you.

---

aw

shawl	str____	cr____l
shawl		
_____	_____	_____
h____k	gn____	dr____
_____	_____	_____

---

ew

vi____	cr____	thr____
_____	_____	_____
n____	bl____	f____
_____	_____	_____

---

ow

pl____	all____	sh____er
_____	_____	_____
t____el	fr____n	p____er
_____	_____	_____

Choose a word from page 44 to finish each phrase

1. not to chew, but to _____

2. not to walk, but to _____

3. not hay, but _____

4. not a cape, but a _____

5. not an eagle, but a _____

6. not to color, but to _____

7. not old, but _____

8. not a sight, but a _____

9. not the captain, but the _____

10. not many, but a _____

11. not caught, but _____

12. not breathed in, but _____ out

13. not a smile, but a _____

14. not a bath, but a _____

15. not a washcloth, but a _____

16. not a shovel, but a _____

17. not weakly, but with _____

18. not to forbid, but to _____

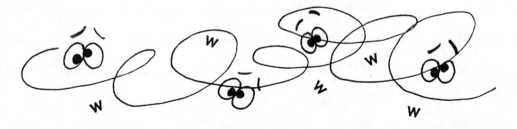

In Perfect Harmony

Add the consonants, **ch**, **ck**, **gh**, **ng**, **sh**, **ph** or **th**, to each group of letters to make a word that matches the clue. Write the word on the line.

1. lau __ __ (a happy noise) _____

2. fif __ __ (one of 5 equal parts) _____

3. it __ __ (a prickly skin feeling) _____

4. qui __ __ (not slow) _____

5. sti __ __ (''bite'' of a bee) _____

6. clo __ __ (fabric or material) _____

7. sear __ __ (look for) _____

8. dea __ __ (not birth) _____

9. gra __ __ (a kind of chart) _____

10. thi __ __ (not thin) _____

11. enou __ __ (as much as needed) _____

12. cru __ __ (to smash) _____

13. stro __ __ (not weak) _____

14. spri __ __ (not autumn) _____

15. swit __ __ (to change with another) _____

Circle the words from page 46 in the wordsearch below. Look across, down, diagonally, and backwards. As you find each word, write it on a line.

s	h	l	a	u	g	h	t	o	l	c
t	e	a	l	n	h	t	h	k	i	u
i	n	a	i	u	q	f	c	h	r	a
n	o	r	r	d	u	i	t	c	h	l
g	p	r	e	c	u	f	h	r	g	s
s	h	a	g	q	h	h	i	u	r	w
c	t	t	f	i	f	u	c	s	a	i
h	b	u	r	t	q	s	k	h	p	t
w	r	o	t	e	n	o	u	g	h	c
t	g	n	s	t	r	o	n	g	i	h

1. _____

2. _____

3. _____

4. _____

5. _____

6. _____

7. _____

8. _____

9. _____

10. _____

11. _____

12. _____

13. _____

14. _____

15. _____

It's About Time

In each group of words, cross out the one that doesn't belong. Then write the other three words on the lines.

hours, now, seconds, minutes

_____ _____ _____

yesterday, tomorrow, awhile, today

_____ _____ _____

whenever, morning, evening, afternoon

_____ _____ _____

Draw a line to match the words that are opposites. Write *both* words on the line.

dawn   after _____

sooner   dusk _____

before   sunset _____

sunrise   later _____

Choose words from above to finish these analogies.

Yesterday is to before, as tomorrow is to _____ .

Seconds are to minutes, as minutes are to _____ .

Morning is to sunrise, as evening is to _____ .

Yesterday is to today, as today is to _____ .

Evening is to dusk, as morning is to _____ .

Complete the puzzle.

ACROSS
4. not before, but...
6. day after today
8. parts of an hour
10. day before today
13. not sooner, but...
14. early part of day, ending at noon
15. when the sun moves below the horizon
16. time just before dark
17. not later, but...

DOWN
1. not after, but...
2. plural of hour
3. beginning of daylight
5. last part of day and early part of night
6. this day
9. when the sun moves above the horizon
11. parts of a minute
12. time between morning and evening

Who's Who at School?

Use the letters on the left to fill in the empty boxes and make school words. (HINT! You will use some letters more than once in a word.)

1. e *and* r   s   c   t a   y

2. i *and* p   r   n c   a l

3. c *and* e   t   a   h   r

4. e *and* t   s   u d   n

5. m *and* c   u s i

6. a *and* r   l i b   i   n

7. e *and* u   n   r s

8. a *and* d   i   e

9. i *and* p   u   l

10. a *and* t   c u s   o d i   n

11. f *and* e   o   i c

12. c *and* o   k

13. c *and* u   l   n   h

14. a *and* s   c l   m   t e

15. a *and* t   j   n i   o r

In each set of parentheses, cross out the word that doesn't make sense. Write the correct word.

1. The school (nurse/pupil) _____ helps you if you are hurt or not feeling well.

2. Our (music/principal) _____ is the leader of our school.

3. Our (librarian/nurse) _____ helps us find good books to read.

4. Our teacher has an (nurse/aide) _____ to help her.

5. Our school's (pupil/secretary) _____ works in the (office/music) _____.

6. The words (student/custodian) _____ and (janitor/cook) _____ mean the same.

7. The person who instructs us is called our (cook/teacher) _____.

8. Our (nurse/cook) _____ works in the (library/lunch) _____ room.

9. (Pupil/music) _____ is another name for (aide/student) _____.

10. My (pupil/classmates) _____ love to go to (music/lunch) _____ class.

Review

Pages 36-39 Circle the misspelled word in each row. Write that word correctly on the line.

stories	terkey	herd	_____
gardan	birth	yard	_____
orchard	north	orenge	_____
protien	people	clay	_____
veil	recieve	eight	_____

Pages 40-41 In each set of parentheses, cross out the incorrect word(s). Write the correct word on the line.

We could (sea/see) _____ (to/too/two)

_____ (bears/bares) _____

looking at a (pare/pair/pear) _____ of

(hour/our) _____ (pear/pair/pare)

_____ trees. They tried stretching (there/

their/they're) _____ bodies to reach the

(pears/pairs/pares) _____ .

Pages 42-43 Add **ed** and **ing** to each word.

enjoy	_____	_____
carry	_____	_____
change	_____	_____

Pages 44-45 Add **aw**, **ew**, or **ow** to complete each word.

h_ _k   p_ _er   vi_ _

sh_ _er   sh_ _l   fr_ _n

all_ _   f_ _   t_ _el

Pages 46-47 Add the correct consonant digraph to make a word. Write the word on the line.

fif_ _ _____   stro_ _ _____

sear_ _ _____   lau_ _ _____

gra_ _ _____   qui_ _ _____

Pages 48-51 Write each word in the correct word boxes.

yesterday

librarian

secretary

morning

student

tomorrow

Buried Treasure

Unscramble the letters to form words from the Word List.

1. a e e l p s _____
2. c d l o s _____
3. a e c m r s _____
4. a f l o t _____
5. d l h o _____
6. b e f i r _____
7. w o n k _____
8. a d o r _____
9. n o s w _____
10. d g l o _____
11. i e e c p _____
12. e i f h t _____
13. a e h t w _____
14. o a s t t _____
15. l o d f _____

Word List				
piece	gold	fold	scream	float
brief	hold	know	wheat	road
thief	scold	snow	please	toast

Use the words from page 54 to finish these analogies.

1. Beans are to peas, as oats are to _____.

2. Summer is to rain, as winter is to _____.

3. Kept is to keep, as held is to _____.

4. Grass is to yard, as pavement is to _____.

5. Down is to up, as sink is to _____.

6. Quiet is to whisper, as loud is to _____.

7. Ruby is to diamond, as silver is to _____.

8. Wrinkle is to crinkle, as crease is to _____.

9. Long is to lengthy, as short is to _____.

10. Right is to praise, as wrong is to _____.

11. Egg is to fry, as bread is to _____.

12. Total is to whole, as part is to _____.

13. Find is to policeman, as steal is to _____.

14. Grew is to grow, as knew is to _____.

15. Frown is to displease, as smile is to _____.

Compound Nouns

Read each clue and pay close attention to the underlined words. Write a compound word that the clue describes.

1. a <u>rope</u> you <u>jump</u> over _____

2. a <u>ball</u> of <u>snow</u> _____

3. <u>corn</u> that will <u>pop</u> _____

4. the <u>day</u> of <u>birth</u> _____

5. a <u>bow</u> of colors in the sky after a <u>rain</u> _____

6. a <u>paper</u> with <u>news</u> _____

7. the <u>end</u> of the <u>week</u> _____

8. when <u>hair</u> is <u>cut</u> _____

9. <u>ground</u> to <u>play</u> on _____

10. mechanical <u>writer</u> to <u>type</u> with _____

11. a <u>nut</u> the size of a <u>pea</u> _____

12. a <u>flake</u> of <u>snow</u> _____

13. a <u>shell</u> by the <u>sea</u> _____

14. a <u>deer</u> that can be harnessed and guided with <u>reins</u> _____

sea + shell = seashell

In each section write the letter to match the two words of each compound word. Write the compound word and then write the number of syllables in that word in the box.

snow __g__	a. deer _____	**snowball** _____	**2**
rein _____	b. paper_____		☐
play _____	c. day_____		☐
sea _____	d. ground_____		☐
news _____	e. nut_____		☐
birth _____	f. shell_____		☐
pea _____	g. ball_____		☐

week _____	a. flake_____		☐
snow _____	b. bow_____		☐
hair _____	c. corn_____		☐
rain _____	d. end_____		☐
jump _____	e. cut_____		☐
type _____	f. rope_____		☐
pop _____	g. writer_____		☐

sea + horse = seahorse

Perplexed by Plurals?

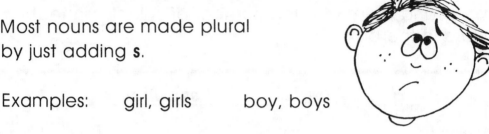

Most nouns are made plural
by just adding **s**.

Examples: girl, girls   boy, boys

Words that end in **s**, **x**, **ch** or **sh**, add **es**. Write the
plural for each of these nouns.

1. dish_____   5. box_____

2. gas_____   6. match_____

3. brush_____   7. boss_____

4. tax_____   8. sandwich_____

Words that end in **y**, preceded by a consonant,
change the **y** to an **i** before adding **es**. Write the
plural for each of these nouns.

9. country_____   11. lady_____

10. party_____   12. glossary_____

Some words that end in **f** (or **fe**), change the **f** (or **fe**)
to **v** before adding **es**. Write the plural for each of
these nouns.

13. knife_____   15. wife_____

14. elf_____   16. half_____

Fill in each blank with the plural form of a word from the Word Box.

| box | sandwich | half | glossary |

1. Mom cut the orange into two _____.
2. Meg and Laura made _____ for the picnic.
3. Many non-fiction books have _____ .
4. We packed our dishes in _____.

| match | lady | knife | brush |

5. The _____ rode to work together.
6. The _____ go next to the spoons.
7. Dad needs _____ to start the campfire.
8. The painter used several different _____.

| tax | wife | boss | party |

9. The men's _____ went sailing.
10. I was invited to two _____ last night.
11. On April 15th, everyone pays their _____.
12. The _____ gave Julie flowers on Secretaries' Day.

| dish | country | gas | elf |

13. Helium and oxygen are both _____.
14. Dad washed the _____ while I dried them.
15. The _____ made shoes for the cobbler.
16. Our trip took us through two _____.

Double Your Pleasure

Complete each word by
adding double consonants.
Then write the word.

1. h a __ __ e r (a tool) _____

2. d e __ __ e r t (after dinner sweets) _____

3. b a __ __ o o n (a party decoration) _____

4. s u __ __ e r (evening meal) _____

5. b l i __ __ a r d (bad snowstorm) _____

6. w i __ __ e r (not the loser) _____

7. s u __ __ e r (not winter) _____

8. s o __ __ y (feeling regret) _____

9. j u __ __ l e (a clown's trick) _____

10. f o __ __ y (cloudlike mist) _____

11. v a __ __ e y (between mountains) _____

12. l e __ __ e r (a note) _____

13. l e __ __ o n (something taught) _____

14. b o __ __ o m (not top) _____

15. c o __ __ o n (a natural fabric) _____

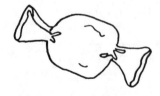

Divide each word between the double consonant and write it on the lines. The first one has been done for you.

1. blizzard	**bliz**	**zard**
2. juggle		
3. cotton		
4. hammer		
5. lesson		
6. winner		
7. balloon		
8. valley		
9. supper		
10. bottom		
11. letter		
12. sorry		
13. dessert		
14. foggy		
15. summer		

HINT! Do you get confused between *dessert* and *desert*? Look at the *ss* in dessert and think that two desserts might be just fine. Then look at the *s* in desert and think that one desert is more than enough for anybody!

Before and After

A prefix is a syllable placed in front of a base word.	A suffix is a letter or syllable added to the end of a base word.
Examples: **a-, dis-, re-, mis-**	Examples: **-ly, -ful, -y, -able, -ed**

Decide if each word in the Word List has a prefix or a suffix. Write it under the correct heading.

Word List

apart	mistake	discover	rewrite
closely	difficulty	personally	comfortable
healthy	around	answered	dishonest
rebuild	suddenly	misspell	forgetful

Words with Prefixes

_____

_____

_____

_____

_____

_____

_____

Words with Suffixes

_____

_____

_____

_____

_____

_____

_____

Use words from page 62 to complete each sentence.

1. Carrots and celery are _____ foods.

2. After proofreading, Jon will _____ his paper.

3. A lot of people _____ the word *misspell*.

4. You need to watch _____!

5. Shawna _____ the question correctly.

6. The children gathered _____ their teacher.

7. Is that chair _____ to sit in?

8. The lightning _____ flashed in the sky.

9. It is _____ to lie, cheat, or steal.

10. Please take the blocks _____ and put them away.

11. Did you make a _____ on your test?

12. When you can't remember things, you're _____.

13. Did the police _____ who did it?

14. Don't take this _____ , but....

15. You will have _____ catching that cat.

16. They'll have to _____ the school because of the fire.

forget + ful = forgetful

Hard or Soft?

The letters **c**, **g** and **s** each have what we call *hard* and *soft* sounds. Write each word from the word boxes under the correct heading.

| cities   cattle   collar   fence   certain   camera |

c has the sound of **k**,
as in carry

_____
_____
_____

c has the sound of **s**,
as in dance

_____
_____
_____

| guide   germ   geometry   grapes   gifts   gentle |

g has the sound of **g**,
as in game

_____
_____
_____

g has the sound of **j**,
as in gym

_____
_____
_____

| subject   sight   girls   measure   special   exercise |

s has the sound of **s**,
as in safe

_____
_____
_____

s has the sound of **z**,
as in his

_____
_____
_____

Circle the misspelled word in each row. Then write that word correctly.

1. cities	sertain	camera	_____
2. subgect	grapes	fence	_____
3. exercise	collar	jentle	_____
4. germ	girls	giude	_____
5. gifts	kamera	geometry	_____
6. speshial	gentle	measure	_____
7. kattle	subject	gifts	_____
8. guide	fence	graips	_____
9. collar	jeometry	sight	_____
10. measure	grils	certain	_____
11. camera	sight	sities	_____
12. special	germ	meazure	_____
13. gurm	exercise	special	_____
14. fense	girls	guide	_____
15. grapes	giffts	cattle	_____
16. sihgt	cattle	subject	_____
17. cities	certain	exercize	_____
18. kollar	gentle	geometry	_____

Readin' 'n' Writin'

In each row, cross out the word that doesn't belong. Write the other words on the line.

novel, fiction, separate _____

personal, noun, verb _____

reading, writing, answer _____

edit, once, proofread _____

favorite, journal, article _____

author, several, poet _____

Choose a word from the Word List to complete each analogy.

Word List

library   dictionary   mystery   cursive

Printing is to manuscript,

as writing is to _____.

Movies are to video store,

as books are to _____.

Recipes are to cookbook,

as definitions are to _____.

Humor is to comedy,

as suspense is to _____.

Write the correctly spelled word from page 66 next to its phonetic spelling.

1. / jûr′ nəl / _____

2. / nŏv′ əl / _____

3. / är′ti kəl / _____

4. / rē′dĭng / _____

5. / ĕd′ ĭt / _____

6. / noun / _____

7. / kûr′ sĭv / _____

8. / rī′ tĭng / _____

9. / vûrb / _____

10. / proof′ rēd / _____

11. / lī′ brĕr ē / _____

12. / fĭk′ shən / _____

13. / mĭs′ tə rē / _____

14. / dĭk′ shə nĕr ē / _____

15. / ô′ thər / _____

16. / pō′ ĭt / _____

JUST FOR FUN! What is the name of your favorite fiction book?

_____

"An Apple a day"

Math 'n' Money

Write each word from the Word List in the correct word boxes.

Word List

addition	penny	money	answer
subtraction	nickel	arithmetic	equal
multiply	quarter	fractions	difference
divide	dollar	decimals	remainder

1.

2.

3.

$$\begin{array}{r} 12 \\ +\ 2 \\ \hline 14 \end{array}$$

4.

5.

6.

7.

8.

9.

10.

11.

12.

$$\begin{array}{r} 10 \\ +\ 5 \\ \hline 15 \end{array}$$

13.

14.

15.

16.

Circle the words from page 68 in the wordsearch below. Look across, down, diagonally, and backwards. As you find each word, write it on a line.

d	i	e	d	i	v	i	d	s	r	a	s	n	a
q	u	e	e	q	u	e	l	u	e	d	r	d	r
u	c	a	c	m	a	t	t	b	m	q	r	f	r
a	d	d	i	t	i	o	n	t	a	e	u	r	a
r	m	s	m	o	n	e	y	r	i	c	m	a	l
t	p	o	a	u	i	e	i	a	n	n	e	c	l
e	n	f	l	r	l	t	r	c	d	e	g	t	o
r	l	t	s	a	h	e	i	t	e	r	h	i	d
e	e	p	e	m	w	m	p	i	r	e	a	o	o
q	k	m	e	s	p	h	l	o	d	f	n	n	l
u	c	t	n	n	t	n	y	n	r	f	m	s	l
a	i	a	r	i	n	m	u	l	t	i	p	l	y
c	n	a	n	r	a	y	l	l	o	d	o	l	l

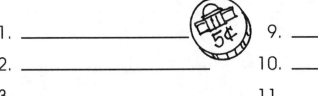

1. _____
2. _____
3. _____
4. _____
5. _____
6. _____
7. _____
8. _____

9. _____
10. _____
11. _____
12. _____
13. _____
14. _____
15. _____
16. _____

Review

Pages 54-55 Circle the letter(s) that make the /ē/ or /ō/ sound.

s n o w	p l e a s e	k n o w
t o a s t	p i e c e	t h i e f
b r i e f	s c o l d	w h e a t

Pages 56-57 Draw a line to match the two parts of each compound word. Then write the words in alphabetical order.

rein	corn	_____
pea	bow	_____
rain	nut	_____
pop	deer	_____

Pages 58-61 Write the plurals for the following words.

box _____   boss _____

balloon _____   elf _____

glossary _____   dish _____

knife _____   letter _____

match _____   party _____

Pages 62-63 Write the base word for each word.

suddenly_____   misspell_____

rebuild_____   comfortable_____

discover_____   forgetful_____

Pages 64-69 Choose a word from the Word List to match each clue below.

Word List		
special	arithmetic	mystery
measure	exercise	answer
noun	divide	journal
author	nickel	certain

1. a daily record _____

2. more than ordinary _____

3. a person who writes novels _____

4. another word for math _____

5. a five-cent piece _____

6. a reply to a question _____

7. to separate something _____

8. for sure _____

9. a part of speech _____

10. something secret or unknown _____

11. to find the size or length _____

12. physical activity; work out _____